Accounting
for Managers

Other titles in the Briefcase Books series include:

To learn more about titles in the Briefcase Books series go to **www.briefcasebooks.com**

You'll find the tables of contents, downloadable sample chapters, information on the authors, discussion guides for using these books in training programs, and more.

Accounting
for Managers

William H. Webster, CPA

McGraw-Hill

New York Chicago San Francisco Lisbon London
Madrid Mexico City Milan New Delhi San Juan
Seoul Singapore Sydney Toronto

This book is printed on recycled, acid-free paper containing a mini-mum of 50% recycled de-inked fiber.

Contents

Preface

A ccounting knowledge is a core business skill that both complements and enhances your other talents. Individuals promoted to management or supervisory roles from either line or staff jobs find that many of their new responsibilities involve knowing something about accounting. Congratulations on your promotion! You've come to the right place to start developing those accounting skills. If you haven't had a recent promotion, more congratulations are in order. You are taking steps to gain the skills that will lead to promotion in the near future.

Your new duties could involve record keeping or report preparation and forwarding the results to the appropriate department. You might also be involved in preparing or analyzing departmental budgets. Maybe you are in sales and have questions about why there isn't more money for travel. Perhaps your company has a profit-sharing plan and you're suddenly intensely interested in how profits are calculated. You could be working in a smaller business where you now have full responsibility for the production function and have to decide where and how to spend the money. Any of these events could trigger your awareness that you need to know something about accounting and how money works in an organization.

You may work for one of the many levels of government or for a nonprofit organization. Although both government and nonprofits have separate accounting rules, most of the same basic functions apply across all the organizational types. I'll touch on some of these differences as we travel through the book.

As you go through this book, you'll find that accounting concepts or information influence almost every decision you will make as a manager. I'm interested in making sure that you finish with an understanding of several key accounting concepts. For this reason, only the most concentrated examples are included here. After finishing this book and working in your job for a while, you may decide to take some accounting courses to practice with detailed examples of the many problems you find in accounting. That's a good idea, particularly as you rise to greater responsibility.

For now, my expectation is that you will learn enough from this book to be able to contribute in internal discussions about accounting issues and questions, use some of the many good tips on making smarter decisions, and enhance your value and productivity for your company or organization. If any questions develop, feel free to visit my Web site, www.mywebcpa.com, or e-mail me at bwebster@mywebcpa.com or bwebcpa@bellatlantic.net.

If your company needs any accounting assistance and is publicly traded, you will probably look to one of the Big Four accounting firms or a major regional firm. If your company is smaller, please consider Fiducial, the international professional services firm with more than 700 U.S. offices and another 350 worldwide. I say this because I own a Fiducial office in Falls Church, Virginia and have seen the difference they can make for small businesses.

Special Features

The idea behind the books in the Briefcase Books series is to give you practical information written in a friendly, person-to-person style. The chapters are relatively short, deal with tactical issues, and include lots of examples. They also feature numerous sidebars designed to give you different types of specific information. Here's a description of the boxes you'll find in this book.

These boxes do just what their name implies: give you tips and tactics for using the ideas in this book to intelligently understand and use accounting to do your job better.

These boxes provide warnings for where things could go wrong when looking at the numbers.

These boxes give you how-to and insider hints for effectively developing and using accounting information.

Every subject has some special jargon, especially accounting. These boxes provide definitions of these terms.

It's always useful to have examples that show how the principles in the book are applied. These boxes provide descriptions of text principles in action.

This icon identifies boxes where you'll find specific procedures you can follow to take advantage of the book's advice.

How can you make sure you won't make a mistake when using accounting data. You can't, but these boxes will give you practical advice on how to minimize the possibility of an error.

Acknowledgments

This book would not have happened without the patience and prodding of John Woods as he endured far too much authorial anguish and the editorial guidance of Robert Magnan, who gave positive leadership. I owe both these gentlemen and other CWL Publishing Enterprises staff my thanks. Early encouragement came from Arkansas State Senator Jim Argue, Jr. who placed the first Amazon order, and Barbara Branyan's review comments. I would also like to thank the many people I interviewed for this book. Among them are Magaret Fidow, Assistant Professor of Accounting at City University of Hong Kong; Susan Armstrong, EA, and Robin Erskine, EA, of Fairfax, Virginia; Terry Steinlicht, MBA, of Hanover, Pennsylvania; Dr. Bart A. Basi, Center for Financial, Legal, and Tax Planning; Bill Morice, CPA, and Maria Riverso of Fiducial; and Andy Martin, CPA, and all the other sharp people in the Fiducial Tax Department. Finally, I want to acknowledge the inspiration and example of Richard Blohm, a man who taught thousands to help tens of thousands.

About the Author

Bill Webster started his accounting practice in 1994, receiving his Enrolled Agent certification in 1996 and CPA in 1998. He is retired from the Federal Aviation Administration after 23 years of federal service as an Air Traffic Control Specialist. His last assignment was program management and implementation of computer systems. Other FAA assignments included a stint as an FAA Academy Instructor in Oklahoma City, Oklahoma and Assistant Manager for Automation in Fort Worth, Texas.

His education includes the MBA program at Humboldt State University, Arcata, California and the MFA program at the University of Southern California, Los Angeles. His BA is in English from Kenyon College. He also holds Certificated Flight Instructor and Commercial Pilot ratings.

How to Speak Accounting

You've heard the saying that nothing happens until someone sells something. After that sale, accounting takes over as the basic activity of business.

The Three Questions

Every business asks three key questions:

- How much money came in?
- Where did the money go?
- How much money is left?

The answer to each question can come only from the practice known as accounting. Like other practices such as medicine and law, accounting has its own vocabulary. In many ways, accounting is the language of business.

Accounting can become quite complex. It has a high MEGO factor. MEGO stands for that state of mental saturation when "My Eyes Glaze Over" in stupefaction. An exasperated student was once overheard complaining, "Who ever thought addition and subtraction could be this hard?"

In the Beginning

Accounting is one of our oldest skills. The earliest collections of understandable writing track how many bushels of grain came into the king's warehouse. From the very beginning of commerce, counting stuff made it possible. That started around 3500-3100 B.C. Those clay tablets also tell who brought in the grain and how much the king took. Tax collecting is an activity closely linked to accounting. We'll learn how crucial that can be to your business health in Chapter 9.

Whatever your responsibilities are in your business or organization, you need accounting skills to perform at your best. If you are in sales, you learn your product's features and how to show them to buyers. Those features include the cost or value proposition and how it affects your customers' buying decisions. Marketing managers study how to find and appeal to a product's target groups. Working up price points can mean some detailed cost analysis. Production managers learn how to plan workflow to control costs. Senior managers use financial statements to speak to those outside about their business's prospects.

Visualize

Many successful managers find it easier to visualize or imagine what they are trying to learn. This technique helps them bridge from the known to the unknown. You'll find several visual image examples used throughout this book to help you see key concepts clearly. Because accounting often deals with numbers and abstractions, it's useful to work with these images as a guide to better understanding.

Whatever your management level, you need to know accounting because your decisions will often be determined by "the numbers." That is how managers keep score and are graded. That's why you bought this book and that's what we're going to give you. Fasten your seat belt. We're taking off!

Visualize to Understand

Start with an aerial view. Imagine your business or organization as a country. It may be a big country or a small one. You may live in a small town or the bustling capital. Your country has mountains and forests, fields and farms, rivers and lakes. Next, imagine that all the cash that comes into your business is water. Water helps your crops to grow. You can dam water to make power to drive your factories. Store the water in lakes to save for the dry season. You can give water to your people to slake their thirst.

That water may come from distant springs high in the mountains. It may come as a river that flows by your door. It may be piped to you across a desert. But it must come to you. And you must manage it.

In the desert colonies of the old Southwest, the Spanish governors set up the *acequia*, or water management system. You can still see its charming canal running through Santa Fe and it is still working, providing water for gardens throughout the city. The canals are called *domos* and the manager is the *majordomo,* or canal manager. It is a very important job. The canals must be kept clean and in good repair, and he organizes this work. In addition, the canal runs through the property of many people. Each is supposed to take water only on a certain day, so that everyone has enough. The majordomo makes sure everyone follows the rules.

An accounting system does for your business exactly what a water-management system does for a city. It makes sure that the money that comes in flows to all the right places. It helps you make sure that you know where the money is. Accounting, or money management, is the art of knowing where the money is and making the right decisions about what to do with it so that your business will grow.

If the money doesn't come in, your business or your organization will die an agonizing death from thirst.

Many of the dot-com start-ups of the late 1990s began with a large pool of venture capital cash. They had high liquidity. The managers, more often than not, spent that money on fancy furniture, equipment, and offices and on heavy advertising, and large salaries. The venture capital cash poured out before any comparable flow of cash came in from customers. The result? All the cash drained away and businesses died of thirst. In Chapter 3, we will cover cash flow. This short example should give you an idea how important it is to manage cash flow. Pay close attention when we get there: this is a lesson that could have kept some dot-coms from turning into dot-bombs. Then, in Chapter 4, we'll cover some ways you can actually measure the liquidity/cash position of your business.

So, the first thing your business needs to become real is cash. How do you get that cash? You can get it from selling things. You can also get it through a loan. Almost all businesses start with a loan, whether from the owner's savings, money collected from friends and family, the basic venture capitalists, or a bank.

Smart Managing

Liquidity Ability to meet current obligations with cash or other assets that can quickly be converted to cash. The more cash, the more liquid. The less cash, the less liquid.

If things don't pan out, you may be able to mournfully bid farewell to your money. Family may be grudgingly forgiving. However, friends and banks have this quaint idea that they want their money back. Therefore, you need a way to track all those loans coming in. Who gave you how much and when? What did you spend the money on? Goods to put on the shelves? The shelves themselves?

Then, a miracle occurs. That first customer or client comes in and gives you cash for what you sell. What do you do with that cash? Buy more goods? More shelves? Pay off your parents? The bank? Things are going to get really complicated really fast. Your accounting system and your understanding of how it works will save you.

Your accounting system is nothing more than a series of locks, lakes, and levees for your cash flow. It's a way of channeling and classifying the cash so that you can start to make some decisions about what to do with it and how to get more of it. You're now doing what a manager does: you're controlling

---

Think like an Owner

Smart Managing

"Wait a minute," you say. "I'm a first-line supervisor in a machine shop. What do I need to know about starting and running a business?" Here's a news flash. The key to becoming a successful manager is to start thinking like an owner. That single attitude adjustment will put you head and shoulders above many, if not most of your peers. You will now start to see the relationships between and among business activities. Make that adjustment and you have earned back the price of this book in multiples of thousands. Of course, the second key is to wait until you've absorbed and practiced the lessons in the rest of this book before telling the CEO how to run the business.

---

and directing resources.

Hold that image of cash as water in your mind for another moment. It can easily evaporate. It can easily trickle away. You now begin to appreciate how important tracking what happens to that cash can be. As a manager you assign resources: people, cash, materials, time. You need some way of knowing where your resources are, what they should be doing, and how well they're doing it.

The Accounting System

You need an accounting system that's the right size to handle the demands of your business. It also has to be well designed so that it gives you the information you need. Many businesses can be managed successfully with nothing more complicated than a checkbook register. As volume increases, however, you may go to a manual system or a computer spreadsheet. Higher volumes and more transactions demand a computerized system. These systems range in price from under $500 to well into seven figures for large organizations.

To start another image in your mind, your accounting system is the plumbing of your business. It is the way you direct, match, and track your resources. What were the sales of Product X? How much time did Bob spend on Project Y? Am I over my travel budget for the year? These answers come from your accounting system. The plumbing in a pup tent is pretty basic. As you move up in complexity, the plumbing in a 1000-square-foot house with one bathroom and one kitchen is simpler than in a mansion with a dozen bathrooms and several kitchens. You want an accounting system that meets your needs.

The information an accounting system provides has two faces—external and internal. To provide these two different views, your accounting system divides into two parts—*financial* accounting and *management* accounting. Each of these areas is a separate discipline in its own right.

Financial accounting is the face your business shows the outside world. Here the daily "gozinta" and "gozouta" become the financial statements that you present to your bank, your stockholders and investors, and taxing authorities. These financial statements are basically historical records that cover a particular time period. It could be yesterday or a year. Each has certain valuable information to help managers make decisions. We will cover financial accounting in Chapters 2, 3, and 4.

Management accounting can be thought of as real-time accounting. It provides the information you need to run your business, and it begins with day-to-day record keeping. Gathering this information on the "gozinta" and "gozouta" forms the basis for many of your managerial decisions. These numbers can be sliced and diced many ways to help you do your job. We'll cover management accounting in Chapters 5, 6, and 7.

> **Key Concepts**
> **Smart Managing** "Gozinta" and "gozouta" are sophisticated accounting terms representing the generic sum of all inputs into an entity and the generic sum of all outputs from that same entity. The smart manager keeps in mind that those liquid assets are just coming into or going out of the business. Those are the basics in accounting.

Accounting from the Bottom Up

We opened this chapter with three questions that every business asks:

- How much money came in?
- Where did the money go?
- How much money is left?

However, to get to the answer to these questions, we need to understand several ideas. We're going to start from the simplest and work our way up to the financial statements that will answer our questions. Our explanation of accounting will also follow history; accounting developed slowly over the last 500 years to the sophisticated computer systems and highly specialized accounting standards we use today.

Double Entry

The first principle of accounting we need to understand is called *double-entry* bookkeeping. Each transaction made in the accounting system is entered twice. No, this does not mean we are keeping two sets of books. We enter every transaction twice, to show where the money comes from and where it is going.

> **Key Term**
>
> **Financial statements** A set of accounting documents prepared for a business that cover a particular time period and describe the financial health of the business.

An Italian monk, Luca Pacioli, gets the credit for developing double entry in 1494, although it first appeared some 50 years earlier. Next time you think you're getting confused by double entry, remember this. It's been around for more than 500 years. Most of the people who used it didn't know how to program VCRs. You are way ahead at the start.

> **Key Term**
>
> **Transaction** Any event that affects the financial position of the enterprise and requires recording. In some transactions, such as depositing a check, money changes hands. But in others, such as sending an invoice to a customer, no money changes hands.
>
> **Account** A place where we record amounts of money involved in transactions. An account shows the total amount of money in one place as a result of all transactions affecting that account.

Key Term

Assets What a business owns or is owed. Examples are real property, equipment, cash, inventory, accounts receivable, and patents and copyrights.

Liabilities What a business owes. Examples are debt, taxes, accounts payable, and warranty claims.

Equity Cash that owners or stockholders have put into the business plus their accumulated claims on the assets of the business. Also known as *owner's equity* or *stockholder's equity*, depending on how the business is organized.

Accounting is concerned with three basic concepts:

- assets
- liabilities
- equity

Let's use a series of T accounts to trace a small job all the way through a business. Let's say you do some work for a customer and you take along a contractor as an assistant. You invoice the client; the client pays. Also, the contractor bills you. How does this look in double-entry bookkeeping, illustrated with T accounts? Let's walk through it one step at a time.

Your customer calls you and asks you to do

TOOLS

T Account

A T account let you visualize both sides of an account. We use T accounts in pairs to set up the double entry. The left side of the T is called the *debit* and right side is the *credit*. Later on, we'll explain why some entries always go on the left and others on the right. Here's a pair of T accounts for writing a check to buy $100 of office supplies.

Assets: Corporate Checking		Expenses: Office Supplies	
Debit	**Credit**	**Debit**	**Credit**
	6/7 $100	6/7 $100	

Notice that we always record a date for each transaction.

the work. You plan the job, put it on the schedule, and arrange for the contractor to come with you. All of this is important business, but none of it shows up in accounting. No transaction has happened yet; if the appointment falls through, you will not get paid anything.

You go and do the work and the contractor comes with you. The customer tells you he is happy with the work and looks forward to receiving your invoice, which he'll pay promptly. The contractor says she'll send you a bill and you promise to pay within one month. Still, no transaction has occurred. If no invoices are sent, and no one gets paid, then it's as if you'd worked for free.

The next day, you write up an invoice for $1,000 and mail it to the customer. The invoice has gone out; now a transaction has occurred. In a pair of T accounts, it looks like this.

Income: Consulting Services		**Assets: Accounts Receivable**	
Debit	**Credit**	**Debit**	**Credit**
	6/2 $1,000	6/2 $1,000	

What do these two diagrams mean?

The first one says that on June 2 the company received $1,000 in income. How is this possible, if you haven't gotten a check yet? Because in accounting, we count the money as coming in when we bill it. Why? Because the money we are owed is an asset and we want to keep track of it. It is of value to our company. We could go to a bank and borrow against the money our customers are due to pay us. So, the value of the company has increased, from an accountant's perspective. The company is

Fixing the Books

Once in a while, we make a mistake. Here's a tip for hunting down that lost entry. Grab a scratch pad and start making T accounts for the ledgers that don't balance or the entry that is partly missing. Make each one carefully. As you work it through, you will see the entry that got missed.

TRICKS OF THE TRADE

worth $1,000 more than the day before, because income has
come in. So we have a credit to income—money coming in.

   The balancing T account is a debit to assets. But if our assets
have increased, why do we debit them? This is one odd aspect
of accounting. Asset accounts are debit accounts. So a debit to
an asset is an increase of money in the company. Later on, we'll
see how this keeps the books in balance.

   But, in double-entry bookkeeping, all transactions are entered twice, so that all accounts are balanced. That is a fundamental rule of accounting.

> **Key Term**
>
> **Debit** A reduction in the amount of money in an account. It shows up on the left side of a T account.
>
> **Credit** An increase in the amount of money in an account. It shows up on the right side of a T account.

If the income account goes
up (is credited) by $1,000, then a debit for $1,000 must show
up somewhere else. It shows up in *Assets—Accounts Receivable,*
as we see in the second T account diagram.

   Accounts receivable is a single account that shows all of the
money that you are owed by everyone. Accounts receivable is
an asset account. That is, it is one of the accounts that show
how much money is in the company.

   The next day, you receive a bill in the mail from your subcontractor. This is another transaction. You enter the bill in your
accounting ledger or system to show that you owe her the
money. The T accounts look like this:

Expenses: Subcontractor		**Liabilities: Accounts Payable**	
Debit	**Credit**	**Debit**	**Credit**
6/3 $200			6/3 $200

   Together, these two T accounts say that your company has
a $200 expense and owes a subcontractor $200. Even though
you haven't paid her bill yet, your company owes the money, so
the value of the company is $200 less than it was.

At the end of the week, you receive a $1,000 check from your customer and deposit it into the corporate checking account. Again, two T accounts record this in your accounting system. These two diagrams may seem backwards. But remember: all asset accounts are debit accounts, so an entry in the debit column is an increase to the account and an entry to the credit column is a decrease.

Assets: Accounts Receivable

Debit	Credit
	6/4 $1000

Assets: Corporate Checking

Debit	Credit
6/4 $1,000	

Now you feel like your business is up and running. You feel so good that you want to pay your subcontractor's bill. Only you can't—the check from the customer hasn't had time to clear the bank. While you're waiting for the check to clear, you ask those three basic questions all managers want to know:

- How much money came in?
- Where did the money go?
- How much money is left?

Since you've entered every transaction, your accounting system should be able to answer those questions. The questions are answered in reports called *financial statements*. The two most important financial statements are the *income and expense statement* and the *balance sheet*.

If you're using a computerized accounting package, you simply go to the

> **Income and expense statement** A document that shows all of the gozinta and gozouta for a business during a particular period of time. Sometimes it is just called an *income statement*. *Revenue* is a synonym for income, so this can also be called a *statement of revenue*.
>
> **Balance sheet** A financial statement that shows the financial position—that is, the assets, liabilities, and value—of a company on a particular day.

Automagic Accounting

Even though all accounting systems are double entry, on many computerized accounting systems we enter each number only once. How does it do that? The computer maintains a chart of accounts. The bookkeeper enters the transaction in one account (say, the bank's checkbook) and then selects another account (perhaps a particular type of expense). When the bookkeeper clicks OK, the transaction is recorded in both accounts. The computer automagically takes care of the second entry, keeping the books in balance. Program instructions also block transactions that do not fit the accounting equation. Try paying your rent out of your insurance account. It won't work.

There are two big advantages of computerized accounting systems. One is that they make it hard to make errors. The other is that you enter the information once, and then see it in several different ways: as data entry screens, account ledgers, and reports.

reports menu, select the report you want, select the start and end dates, and print it out. But, rather than relying on the magic of a computer program, let's walk through the process of build-

Key Term

Chart of accounts A list of all the accounts in the accounting system. Some of them may be used every day, such as Cash, and some rarely or even never.

ing our financial statements, so that you can see how accounting moves from the recording of each transaction to the presentation of useful reports.

Bookkeeping and Accounting

Many people confuse *bookkeeping* and *accounting*. They think that bookkeeping is accounting. Bookkeeping is the act of recording transactions in the accounting system in accordance with the principles discussed in Chapter 2.

Accounting is the way we set up the system, the principles behind it, and the ways we check the system to make sure that it is working properly. Accounting ensures that bookkeeping is honest and accurate and, through financial accounting and management accounting, it provides people outside and inside the business the picture they need of where the company's money is.

Accountants developed bookkeeping procedures as a way to organize records, to classify the many transactions that take place. Bookkeeping puts related transactions together into groups so that their impact on the accounting equation can be recorded and analyzed.

When we put several transactions together into one account, we're creating a *ledger*. Each account has a ledger that lists all its transactions. Every transaction is entered twice, in two ledgers, once as a credit and once as a debit. The individual lines in a ledger are called *entries*. In a manual system, each entry is first put on a master page called the *journal,* or *book of first entry,* and then copied to the appropriate individual account pages. As a result, the books stay in balance; the total of all credits equals the total of all debits.

> **Right from the Start**
>
> If you are a sole proprietor, you may be doing much of your bookkeeping yourself. If so, you might consider taking a bookkeeping course. If someone else is doing it, either inhouse or outside, recognize that it's critical that the initial entries go in correctly. Running down bookkeeping entry mistakes is a tedious task, especially if they happen regularly.

> **Key Term**
>
> **Ledger** The record of all transactions in a particular account. The detail generally includes the date the transaction took place, the amount, whether it was a debit or a credit, and a short memo, if necessary.
>
> **Entry** An individual line in a ledger.
>
> **Journal** Where a transaction is first entered. It's also called the *book of first entry*. While the ledger shows all the action in a particular account, the journal shows the original transaction and all the accounts affected by it. A $1,000 dollar payment could be $250 of fuel, $75 of oil, and $675 of maintenance. The date, the accounts debited and credited, and the memo are also recorded.

Before we overload you with more accounting terminology, let's use the example of our new service business to show how all this works. As a result of the three transactions we've entered, here are the ledgers for five accounts:

Income: Consulting Services

Debit	Credit	Notes
	6/2 $1000	Invoice for consulting services
	$1,000	Total

Assets: Accounts Receivable

Debit	Credit	Notes
6/2 $1,000		Invoice for consulting services
	6/4 $1000	Check received
	0	Total

Assets: Corporate Checking

Debit	Credit	Notes
6/4 $1,000		Check received
$1,000		Total

Liabilities: Accounts Payable

Debit	Credit	Notes
	6/3 $200	Bill received
	$200	Total

Expenses: Subcontractor

Debit	Credit	Notes
6/3 $200		Bill received
$200		Total

- Income: Consulting Services
- Assets: Accounts Receivable
- Assets: Corporate Checking
- Liabilities: Accounts Payable
- Expenses: Subcontractor

With these five account ledgers laid out, we can trace the transactions related to that one day of work. For example, we can see that accounts receivable increased by $1,000 when we sent the invoice, then decreased back to zero when we received the invoice and deposited the check.

Take a moment to trace all the entries from the previous pages in these ledgers. In fact, take more than a moment. Visualize the action that was taken related to each transaction. See yourself first writing an invoice, then receiving and entering a bill, and finally receiving and depositing a check. Find the two entries related to each of these actions. When it's all clear in your mind, you're ready for the big leap—from bookkeeping to accounting.

Financial Statements

After just one job, it's pretty easy to understand the accounts in the ledger. But when we've entered dozens, hundreds, or even thousands of transactions—think how many customers come into a restaurant every day—we need reports that show us what's going on. Looking at the account ledgers would just make our eyes pop out and give us a headache.

First, let's look at the income and expense statement for our company:

Revenues	
Contracting Services	$1,000
Revenue (gross income)	$1,000
Expenses	
Subcontractor	$200
Net Income	$800

The income and expense statement shows details and totals of income accounts and expense accounts. Note that it does not show individual journal entries. From this report, we don't know if we did one job or three jobs—just that the total was $1,000 of contracting jobs billed. *Revenue* or *gross income* is all the money that has come in, without considering expenses. *Net income* is gross income less total expenses; that is, it's the amount of money we've made after expenses. Net income is a key factor in business success. When we're spending more than we're making, that money is a negative number, called *net loss*.

The income and expense statement is useful, but it doesn't show the whole picture. For example, it doesn't tell us how much money we have in the bank account or even whether or not we've paid our subcontractor. To get the rest of the picture, we need a balance sheet.

Assets	
Accounts Receivable	0
Corporate Checking	$1,000
Total Assets	$1,000

Liabilities	
Accounts Payable—	
Subcontractor	$200
Total Liaabilities	$200

Equity	$800

Now we see that, even though we have $1,000 in the checking account, we owe $200 to someone, so our company is worth only $800. In simple terms, *equity* is the financial value, or worth, of a company.

Accounting Principles

Do you remember the scene from the end of *The Wizard of Oz* where the great big voice says, "Pay no attention to that man behind the curtain!"? Accounting is kind of like that. Behind all the terms and rules and reports, there are a few levers and gears that keep the whole thing working. In this chapter, we're taking you behind the scenes. You've already learned the most basic principle—double-entry bookkeeping to keep the books in balance. Let's look at a few more.

- All accounts are assigned a type. These are the most basic types of accounts:
  - income
  - expense
  - asset
  - liability
  - equity
- Each type of account has a normal balance, a side of the T account where normal entries (that increase the account balance) are made.
  - Asset and expense accounts are *debit* accounts, with normal entries that increase account value on the right side of the T account.
  - Liability, equity, and income accounts are *credit* accounts, with normal entries that increase account value on the left side of the T account.
- Income and expense statements always have a period, from a beginning date to an ending date.
- Balance sheets have a single date, reporting the status of the company on that date.
- An income and expense statement shows the change in the balance sheet from the start date to the end date of the income and expense statement.

Normal balance The balance an account is usually expected to have, the side on which an account increases. (The word "normal" here means usual.) Having income as a credit account and expenses as a liability account is logical. But the balance sheet accounts seem to be reversed logically—asset accounts are debited and liability and equity accounts are credited. Yes, this is backwards. This "crossing of the wires" is the trick behind the scenes that makes all the accounts balance.

> **Getting a Handle on Financial Statements**
>
> Tracing changes in the balance sheet to the income and expense statement is more than just an exercise. It is the fastest way to get a handle on accounting. Sure, the first few times, it feels like you're banging your head against a wall. But keep at it. A good manager will check over his or her financial statements every month or at least every quarter. Once you understand them, financial statements help you keep the pulse of your business. If you look at them regularly, they also help you see changes as they happen, so you can catch problems before they become too big to handle.

In our example, the company started on June 1, 2003, with no assets or liabilities in each account. Can you trace every item on the balance sheet for June 5, 2003 to an item on the income and expense statement for June 1 to 5, 2003 (called "month-to-date")?

The Fundamental Equations of Accounting

The preceding sections of this chapter have shown you the gears and wires behind the scenes that make everything work. Now, we are ready for the show: this is how accounting answers the three big questions we introduced at the beginning of the book:

- How much money came in?—revenue or gross income
- Where did the money go?—expenses
- How much money is left?—net income

The Income Equation

We find the direct answer to these three questions on the income and expense statement. The *income statement equation*—revenue – expenses = net income—is the key to the income statement. The result here is simple arithmetic: revenue (the gozinta) minus expenses (the gozouta) yields net income.

The Balance Sheet Equation

The balance sheet answers another set of crucial questions for a company. Today, what is my company worth? What's in my bank account? How much money do other companies or people owe me? How much money do I owe other people or companies?

The fundamental equation of accounting underlies the balance sheet. It looks like this:

assets = liabilities + equity

assets − liabilities = equity

assets − equity = liabilities

The physical layout of the balance sheet matches the first equation:

assets = liabilities + equity

This makes logical sense: the value of what the company owns (assets) minus the value of what the company owes (liabilities) leaves you with what the company is worth (equity).

The Equations and the Normal Accounts

This table illustrates how the income equation balances if we enter our transactions properly on the normal side of each account.

Revenue		−	Expenses	=	Net Income
Debits	**Credits**		**Debits**	**Credits**	
Decrease	Increase		Increase	Decrease	
	Normal Balance		Normal Balance		

This table illustrates how the balance sheet equation—that is, the fundamental equation of accounting—balances properly if we enter our transactions on the normal side of each account.

Assets		=	Liabilities		+	Owner's Equity	
Debits	**Credits**		**Debits**	**Credits**		**Debits**	**Credits**
Increase	Decrease		Decrease	Increase		Decrease	Increase
Normal Balance				Normal Balance			Normal Balance

Every transaction we enter follows the basic accounting equations. In fact, the T accounts are designed to make sure that we follow the equations. That is why some accounts are credit accounts and others are debit accounts.

If each entry is balanced, then all of the entries are balanced and our balance sheet and income statement will come out right. If there is an error in one transaction, it will show up because our financial statements will be out of balance.

The Advantages of an Accounting System

It's possible to run a business on a checkbook. However, you gain a lot by setting up a simple, appropriate accounting system. The reports an accounting system generates let you do these things much more easily than you can if you just keep a checkbook.

- **Find errors.** If a transaction is missing or entered wrong, the books will be out of balance.
- **Plan for the future.** Seeing the gozinta, the gozouta, and what you've got, you can figure out what you're going to need—when to borrow money and what work to do to improve your business.
- **Stop fraud and theft.** If you know your business and your books, you can find out if people are cheating.
- **Get financing.** A good set of books impresses bank loan officers and investors.
- **Make taxes easy.** If you have just a checkbook and shoe-boxes full of receipts, tax time can be a nightmare. It can actually cost less to keep good books all year than to clean up the mess just for the IRS.

A Few Important Details

There are a few more details of the wires and gears behind the scenes that we should mention before we close the chapter.

Getting into the T Account Habit

If you want to learn bookkeeping and accounting quickly—and keep your errors down to a minimum—keep this cheat sheet close to you and memorize it well. Routine transactions usually get applied to standard accounts the same way almost every time. Here are the most common ones.

Transaction	Account 1	Account 2
Invoicing a client	Asset: Accounts Receivable	Income
Depositing a client's check	Asset: Checking Account	Asset: Accounts Receivable
Receiving a bill	Expense (appropriate category)	Liability: Accounts Payable
Paying a bill	Liability: Accounts Payable	Asset: Checking Account (enter on right side, debit, as you are reducing account balance)
Buying supplies by check	Expense (appropriate category)	Asset: Checking Account (enter on right side, debit, as you are reducing account balance)
Buying an asset by check	Asset: Equipment	Asset: Checking Account (enter on right side, debit, as you are reducing account balance)
Buying supplies by credit card	Expense (appropriate category)	Liability: Credit Card (enter on right side, debit, as you are reducing account balance)
Paying a credit card in full by check	Liability: Credit Card (enter on left side to increase account balance to zero)	Asset: Checking Account (enter on right side, debit, as you are reducing account balance)

Compound Entries and Split Accounts

Sometimes, we write one check for several items. This requires a more complex entry: our accounts still balance, but they are spread out over several transactions, not just two.

We'll illustrate this with a general journal entry for a check that was written to an office supply store. Let's say we bought a printer, ink cartridges, and supplies for the annual Christmas party.

The PR column stands for *posting reference*. We use a checkmark in the PR column to indicate that the item has been entered on the separate accounting page in our ledger for that particular account and that it has been checked.

This simple example illustrates the advantages of an accounting system over trying to run a business on a check-book. Imagine seeing a check for $600 for office supplies six months later and wondering, "What in the world did I spend all that money on?" You start digging. With your accountant's help (at $50/hour) you find the receipt. You discover what you paid

Date	Account and Explanation	PR	Debit	Credit
12/10/0x	Asset: Computer Equipment (Printer)		$250	
	Expense: Office Supplies (Ink)		$50	
	Expense: Office Party		$300	
	Asset: Checking—Check #105 paid to The Office Store			$600

for. Your accountant says, "Gee, I wish I'd seen this before we did your taxes. We treated it all as expenses, but the computer printer really is an asset." And you're wondering, "What in the world was I thinking, spending $300 on an office party!"

Long experience has led to a standardized chart of accounts for many businesses. All the accounting software packages come with a built-in chart of accounts, often several.

Key Term

Posting reference (PR) column A column in journals where ledger account numbers are entered when entries are posted to those ledger accounts. The number in the PR column serves two purposes: it gives the ledger account number of the account involved and it indicates that the posting has been completed for the entry.

How Fine a Sieve?

⚠ CAUTION!

One damaging mistake new managers make is to try and break every transaction down into its most basic atomic elements. If you go below three layers, you've almost certainly gone too far, unless you work for a very, very large organization. You may want to have an account for Computers and then break that down into Computers: Hardware and Computers: Software. There may even be a need to break the Software account down into, say, Accounting Software and Scheduling Software. Beyond that you create problems for whoever will be recording the transactions and whoever must build the information back up to analyze. You also create a complex structural system that invites error. As in all things, Keep It Simple, Señor/Señora/Señorita.

You may only need to put in the name of your bank for the cash account. Make adjustments as necessary so that your accounting system returns the information you need to make effective decisions. The bookkeeping system is a tool. It should not be your master.

Cash vs. Accrual

As you can see, an accounting system offers a great deal more than a simple checkbook. There are two basic approaches to accounting; you'll want to choose one for your business. The two approaches are *accrual basis* and *cash basis.*

In this chapter, our example used accrual accounting. You can recognize accrual accounting because you see an asset category called accounts receivable and you see short-term liabilities for bills you need to pay. You can see how valuable accrual accounting is for the internal management

Key Term

Accrual basis An accounting method that tracks income when you send an invoice, even before you receive payment, and tracks expenses when an invoice comes in, even before you pay it.

Cash basis An accounting method that tracks income when you receive the checks or cash and tracks expenses when you make payments.

of your business. It keeps you from being fooled by a big balance in your checking account when you have lots of bills to pay. It also lets you know when business is starting to pick up, as accounts receivable goes up even before the money comes in, and it helps you with collections. In addition, accrual accounting gives you a special report of accounts receivable called the *aging report* that shows you who owes you money—and how late they are in paying it. We will talk more about accrual and cash basis in Chapter 2.

At this point you may feel a bit like you've been "rode hard and put up wet," as we say in South Texas. I just wanted to get past the fear factor as quickly as possible. We'll look at these concepts further as we navigate through the other general concepts of accounting, financial and management accounting, taxes, accounting systems, financial ratio analysis, and auditing. But that should not be difficult, since you now understand the basics. Believe me, you've got it licked. It's all downhill from here.

> **Key Term**
>
> **Aging report** A list of accounts receivable amounts by age. The report is usually divided into columns by 30-day increments, such as 0-30, 31-60, 61-90, 91-120, and 120+. It shows any customers that are slow to pay and reveals problems with collecting on accounts.

Manager's Checklist for Chapter 1

❑ There are three basic questions you ask as a manager—How much money came in? Where did the money go? How much money is left? You'll be a better manager if you think like an owner and keep the big picture in mind.

❑ Because accounting can get dry, it helps to visualize the concepts to see the underlying dynamics. Thinking of cash as water is a useful tool to help understand the ways you can use an accounting system.

❏ Double-entry bookkeeping keeps the books in balance.

❏ We illustrate double-entry bookkeeping by writing transactions in T accounts. The left side of the T is always a debit. The right side is always a credit. Depending on where the account is classified within the equation elements, an increase or a decrease could be either a debit or a credit. For each transaction, the total debits equal the total credits.

❏ The accounting system is based on a chart of accounts that establishes all of the pots where you're going to record transactions.

❏ The complete details of each transaction are recorded in the general journal. Each account in the chart of accounts has its own ledger. A running balance is often kept in these account ledgers.

❏ The statement of revenue, also called the income and expense statement, shows how much money came in, where the money went, and how much money is left over a given period of time. It's based on the equation *revenue – expenses = net income.*

❏ The balance sheet shows you how much money the company is owed, how much it has, how much it owes, and how much it is worth. It expresses the fundamental equation of accounting.

❏ The accounting equation—assets = liabilities + equity—is the foundation of any accounting system. It assigns an increase component and a decrease component to each element of the accounting equation, establishing normal balances for the increase of each type of account.

.

Concepts and Principles, Checks and Balances

The double-entry innovation to track the increase and decrease of each part of the accounting equation (assets = liabilities + equity) made recording business transactions more manageable. There were still several complications. How do you present the information you've recorded? How does an Amsterdam merchant convince a Venetian banker to back the ships sailing for Java? It's a bit impractical to drag out your set of double-entry ledgers for each of your 250 accounts. Even the general journal recording each transaction as it took place is too much. How can you structure this mass of financial information order to make a decision?

Over time, the accounting profession in the United States developed a series of standards that add uniformity to financial statements. These standards are called Generally Accepted Accounting Principles (GAAP). GAAP provides a common language. The users of financial statements feel secure that the numbers in statements issued in New York can be compared with numbers issued in California. This common language of

---

Foreign Practices

The environment in which businesses develop and operate influences accounting principles, concepts, rules, etc. That includes culture: each country's cultural traits will affect the development of its Generally Accepted Accounting Principles. Islam proscribes charging interest. The Swiss desire for secrecy and the lack of large numbers of individual investors have prompted much less disclosure in their financial statements. The Japanese cultural trait for cooperation and the existence of interlocking directorships has influenced the type and amount of information that must be revealed or not revealed to the general public.

---

accounting allows investors to make informed choices without having to learn a new set of accounting rules for each investment considered.

While GAAP is a constant within the United States, these principles are not discovered through scientific research. GAAP is not like the laws of physics, transgressed at peril of death. Experience, application, and observation led to general acceptance that these principles helped meet the objectives of financial accounting and reporting. In setting these standards, accountants asked the question, "What are the objectives of financial accounting information in the U.S.?" The answer was that accounting was to provide full disclosure to actual and potential investors and creditors. The United States developed a type of capitalism that brought it many individual investors. The accounting system that developed could feed those users the data needed to make informed decisions.

As GAAP is the product of several committees, it's not always internally consistent or applied uniformly. Nonetheless, GAAP represents the best collective thinking on the underlying assumptions driving the presentation of financial data. The goal is to publish the quality information needed to make meaningful decisions. These basic GAAP requirements apply to most financial statements. There are other GAAP and accounting requirements that come into play in more technical circumstances. These are appropriate subjects for advanced study.

Key Term **Securities and Exchange Commission (SEC)** A government agency that—through the Securities Act of 1934, the Securities Exchange Act of 1935, the Sarbanes-Oxley Act of 2002, and other legislation—plays a major role in the oversight and enforcement of accounting rules, with the Financial Accounting Standards Board and the Government Accounting Standards Board.

Financial Accounting Standards Board (FASB) A private entity, established in 1973, that issues accounting and financial reporting guidelines like GAAP for the private sector.

Government Accounting Standards Board (GASB) A private entity that sets financial standards for government, including state and local entities, public schools, hospitals, utilities, universities, etc. Many non-governmental organizations also follow GASB pronouncements.

American Institute of Certified Public Accountants (AICPA) The dominant national organization of accountants, through its standards and accreditation procedures. AICPA endorses adherence to FASB and GASB pronouncements. If you work with a CPA, either within or outside the company, you will hear about GAAP.

Closing the GAAP

Table 2-1 provides a summary of GAAP pronouncements.

Quality	Assumptions	Principles	Constraints
relevance	separate entity	cost	materiality
reliability	monetary unit	revenue recognition	cost/benefit
comparability	continuity	matching	prudence
consistency	time period	full disclosure	industry peculiarities

Table 2-1. GAAP fundamentals

The Four Qualitative Characteristics of Information

- relevance
- reliability
- comparability
- consistency

Overall the *cost/benefit quality* of information states that the benefits of accounting and reporting should exceed the cost. It makes no sense to gather, record, process, publish, and analyze information if it costs more to do that than the output is worth.

The primary information qualities are *relevance* and *reliability*.

All information is *relevant* to the original record of the transaction. All financial transactions should be recorded, even the purchase of a postage stamp. At the same time, that level of detail is not needed to present meaningful information in financial statements. For a financial statement presentation, the relevant information is an accurate summation of activities that is timely and has predictive value. Management can also use that information as feedback to analyze business activity.

The information presented must be *reliable*, that is, objective and verifiable. When GAAP is not observed, the reliability of the information becomes increasingly suspect. Offering the financial data to outside scrutiny, as in an audit, can enhance reliability.

The two secondary qualitative aspects are *comparability* and *consistency*.

Comparability means that business activities can be matched, that revenue for one business is the same as revenue for another.

Consistency requires that activities be treated the same over time. Business and external forces can cause the treatment of certain items to vary over time. Recent bad faith charges have often fixated on charges of inconsistency. For this reason, the concept of consistency is receiving greater emphasis. Every business has wide discretion under general GAAP guidelines to treat certain transactions differently. For example, a business can chose different depreciation strategies or ways to account for marketing expenses. Booking full contract income after delivering a beta product is an example on the revenue side.

Within the range of discretion, the company should use the same treatment year after year. Changing the depreciation percentages or amortizing marketing expenses can cause income to seem greater than it actually is. If an error is discovered, the consistency hobgoblin cannot shield the need to correct the error. If it becomes necessary to change the method or the rates being charged, then the financial statements must show a note for that period. The note must state why the change was made and what effect it has on the results.

The Four Assumptions

- separate entity
- monetary unit
- continuity
- time period

Each economic *entity* needs its own financial records. A large company may have several divisions, product lines, and plants whose economic activities are combined in the company financial statements. Within that company, a specific entity, branch, office, or shop must record every economic act. Within the records, each act must be traceable to the appropriate entity. Businesses are making progress in this area. In government, it is still a subject ripe for reform.

The second assumption is *monetary unit.* The economic entity records only quantifiable monetary transactions. For example, hiring a coach who leads the team to a Super Bowl results in tremendous economic benefits to the franchise, but the salary package is the only transaction on the books.

CAUTION!

Don't Mix Personal with Business

A favorite of small and large business owners and officers is recording personal liabilities in the record of company expenses. Any numbers of high-flying CEOs have been tripped up by this supposed stratagem. The practice violates the entity assumption. There are, as in many areas of accounting, gray areas where what might be considered personal expenses, when incurred in relation to a business event, can be valid. See a tax advisor or other expert if there's any question. As a general rule, don't dip your cookie in the company's coffee.

Similarly, the lost opportunity cost in the dashed expectation of the rookie quarterback cannot be written off as an expense; only the eight-figure bonus package can be deducted. The monetary transactions must be reported in a single, stable currency. International companies often report in U.S. dollars (USD), even though their activities span the globe.

Continuity is also known as the *going concern* assumption. The business is expected to last over time. In U.S. law, corporations are seen as individuals with an indefinite life span. Therefore, financial statements can view certain assets and liabilities as long-term, lasting more than a year.

Recall that when we post to the general journal, we always record the date. The *time period* assumption recognizes that business activities take place over time. Financial performance then can be reported and compared for any period of time. The economic impact of buying raw material for manufacture of a product differs from the financed purchase of the machine that makes the product. The raw material is a current asset while it is in inventory and a current expense when it turns into the product. The machine represents a long-term asset and the debt financing is a long-term liability. The time frame in which the report is prepared must take these differences into account in stating the results.

What's Current?

Smart Managing

The term "current" is used a lot in accounting circles. It can be confusing, because the word has various meanings. Here are some examples:

- **Current value:** value at the present time.
- **Current assets:** assets that will be sold, used up, or turned into cash within the current accounting period, usually one year—e.g., cash, accounts receivable, supplies, and merchandise inventory.
- **Current liabilities:** debts that are due for payment within one year—e.g., accounts payable, salaries payable, sales tax payable, and the current portion of notes payable.

The Four Principles

- cost
- revenue recognition
- matching
- full disclosure

The *cost* principle requires that assets appear on the books at the acquiring cash value. Even though a building or land may have substantially increased in value, it is still recorded at the historical cost. This condition explains how the reported "book" value of a company can often be lower than its actual value. Conversely, inflated purchase prices can hide problems in a shaky balance sheet.

The next principle is *revenue recognition*. Under GAAP, the company recognizes revenue only when it is earned upon product delivery or service completion. It seems straightforward that a furniture store recognizes revenue when it sells a table to a customer in July. When does the wholesaler recognize the revenue? In April, when it receives the order? In May, when it delivers the table? In June, when the furniture store pays the bill? The answer is May, when it delivers the product.

Consider the more complicated case of a construction company over the long course of erecting a building. The company needs cash from its customer to pay the ongoing costs of construction. GAAP has industry specific guidelines on activities like progress payments to accommodate special needs of unique business activities.

The *matching* principle measures the performance of the gozinta and gozouta for each time period. The costs of doing business, the expenses, in the period are matched to the revenues generated. Revenues earned less expenses incurred equals income. Income is the measure of performance for the period.

The *time period* assumption often makes measuring and matching revenues and expenses a chore. At the end of the

> ## When Recognition Doesn't Match
>
> **⚠ CAUTION!**
>
> Actions surrounding the twin principles, revenue recognition and matching, have led to some of the greatest displays of stupidity and/or cupidity in the history of financial reporting. Putting expenses into a different time period or reporting revenue when a contract is signed are typical ploys to either pump up or flatten income.
>
> In pilot training, there's a washout test to measure depth perception where two objects have to be lined up at a point. If you can't focus correctly, the two objects stay apart—you don't make the cut. Holding to these two GAAP principles is a test of ethical depth perception. A substantial number of financial scandals would be avoided if managers could make this cut.
>
> It's also important not to attribute to malice that which can be explained by stupidity. Stay smart. Read more books. You heard it here first!

chosen period, many transactions can be at various stages of completion. Income or loss can be hard to measure. The preparer must make assumptions as to the eventual outcome of these transactions. For example, all accounts receivable may be uncollected at the end of the period. The preparer must estimate how much of the receivables can be collected. Inventory is another area subject to estimate and error. How much year-end inventory will be sold in future periods? In addition, estimates must be made as to wages owed, taxes owed, etc. Matching these estimates to the facts of the case often requires sound judgment.

The *full disclosure* principle states that financial information should be complete and accurate for past transactions. There may also be external events, such as a pending lawsuit, or internal events, such as a union action, that would affect the firm's financial health. Even if there's no verifiable economic impact at present, these events should be noted in footnotes to the financial reports. Also, financial transactions between company officers and managers, such as loans, must be noted.

The Four Constraints

- materiality
- cost/benefit
- prudence
- industry peculiarities

The *materiality* constraint is often misunderstood. It does not apply while recording cash transactions. Even small amounts must be recorded. As a general rule, every cash transaction has to be recorded in the general journal.

If you want to alienate the Accounting Department, ask them to track down a $3.13 difference in the balance sheet. The trick, of course, is to discriminate between the trivial and the significant. What is the relative importance of the question? A $1,000 difference may not be worth the cost to correct to a company grossing $100M. To a company grossing $100K, it's worth finding out the problem.

Materiality does not hold when errors of principle are found that need correction. Let's say you learn that a capital item has been erroneously expensed or a different method of depreciation has been applied to a particular asset. The error should be corrected immediately. The concept of materiality cannot be a defense for not correcting errors.

Materiality just means that any of the aforementioned principles can be disregarded if there's no discernible effect on the people who will use the financial information. Note that I'm not suggesting that fraud or carelessness in handling money is acceptable.

The *cost/benefit* constraint kicks in when the company tries to correct the $1,000 error mentioned above. What did it cost Captain Queeg to find out what happened to the strawberry preserves? How hard should the Defense Department look for a missing $100M? You decide whether it's worth it.

Accountants and managers make many estimates. How much to reserve for warranty repairs? How much to set aside for uncollectible accounts? How long will a machine be in productive service? In reporting financial data, they should follow the *prudence* constraint. This means that when two outcomes are equally probable, the less optimistic should be reported. Better to understate than to overstate. So, when the new credit manager reports that the historic rate of 10% uncollectible accounts can be cut to 5% under enlightened leadership, stick with a 10% reserve allowance for doubtful accounts.

Because of fluctuations in several areas above, many industries have generally accepted accounting methods that are in clear contradiction with GAAP. When the use is of information benefit and a clear precedent, its use is acceptable in that industry. An example would be how depletion allowances are treated in the extraction industries.

An additional GAAP requirement is that companies use accrual basis accounting. To apply the various principles, cost, time period, matching, revenue recognition, and others, GAAP mandates the use of accrual basis accounting. Accrual is designed to capture the financial aspects of each economic event as it occurs. Concerns of cash flow, or when the cash actually changes hands, are not relevant to the actual event. Those transactions are recorded separately in the accounts receivable and payable transactions.

Save a Little Money

TRICKS OF THE TRADE

Accrual basis accounting reflects a truer picture of your financial situation than the traditional cash basis accounting. In cash basis, revenues and expenses are recognized only when cash or its equivalent changes hands. The disadvantage in accrual basis is that the Internal Revenue Service (IRS) computes tax due on the reported net income. Thus, an accrual basis entity could pay cash tax on income that it has not yet received. What happens then if the customer defaults?

The U.S. tax code and GAAP have several provisions for taking some of the sting out of this situation. At most, you are out the opportunity cost, and some interest, from having to pay the tax. Still, many small businesses stay on cash basis accounting as long as they are eligible, to avoid paying tax on money they haven't received. Check with your tax advisor to learn if you are eligible. Hint: if you carry inventory or gross in seven figures, probably not.

Zen Accounting

To the novice, accounting often looks like a street corner shell game. The accountant places a pea under one of three walnut shells. He then moves the three shells swiftly over the felt table-top while saying a bunch of magic words like "financial ratios transfer to the balance sheet while the equity pie becomes an expense to third parties," claps his hands, and steps back with a smile. You gingerly lift shell after shell to discover that 1) the pea is not where you thought it was, 2) the pea has magically become two peas, or 3) the pea has disappeared entirely.

This discussion of GAAP shows that there are reasons for the apparent contradictions and inconsistencies. In an ideal world, the typical financial statement is the product of several

---

Identify GAAP Concerns

In November, a public U.S. company that reports on a calendar fiscal year, with manufacturing plants in Maryland and Mexico, has to record economic activity in two currencies. It purchases for cash and immediate delivery machines to make more widgets for both factories. Based on historical maintenance data, the firm plans to use the Maryland machine for seven years and the Mexico machine for five. It signs a contract and accepts a cash down payment to deliver widgets to one customer in a year and signs a second contract to deliver widgets to another customer in six months, but at a much higher price. The Engineering Department that selected the new machines predicts a rate of 10,000 widgets per month, based on machine specifications. The Production Department projects 7,000 widgets per month, based on the training requirements. Purchasing says the price of widget raw materials is going up.

Which of these decisions have GAAP implications? All of them! Decisions like how to record revenues and expenses (in two currencies, no less), how to handle depreciation on the machines, how to show the contracts in the financial statements due out in January, and whether those statements talk about the forward risk of price increases. If third parties use your financial statements to make financial decisions about your business, GAAP requirements seep into every aspect of those statements.

carefully considered competing and, in some cases, mutually exclusive activities. Wise judgment has considered the competing claims and resulted in the most accurate picture of the firm's financial condition.

Many situations develop where two or more GAAP concepts either overlap or contradict. There is no right or wrong answer to these conundrums. Much depends on the volume and nature of the transaction and the industry practices to which they relate. As a manager, you have to decide for yourself whether you'll perform ethically. Be secure that the vast majority of managers are ethical. Bad managers, like airplane crashes, still draw headlines. When they don't, it's time to get very worried.

Checks and Balances

The sudden implosion of many companies at the dawn of the Third Millennium was not a repudiation of GAAP. It was a breakdown in the system of checks and balances that supported GAAP. Even governmental and charitable organizations were infected.

The revenue recognition principle still applies, even though companies reported as current income cash they would not receive for several years. The consistency principle was routinely violated as depreciation schedules were strung out over several years, falsely lowering expenses and thus increasing income. The prudence principle flew out the window as the wildest revenue forecasts drove investors to a fury. Managers, in collusion with their auditors, mocked the full disclosure principle as they reported nonexistent income and hid liabilities behind offshore partnership shells.

Yes, these have been some hard times for managers and accountants—and harder for lots of investors. As a manager, you should understand the temptations that will be placed before you. If you work in a public company, the pressure on quarterly earnings can crush you like a bug if you don't meet your numbers. If you work for a privately held firm, bankers and taxing authorities will show great interest in your financial reports.

By providing a check on unscrupulous managers, the audit function should stop the sort of abuses that have resulted in corporate scandal. The audit function failed in most cases through personal cupidity on the part of auditors rather than structural flaws in the audit process.

Your business should have two types of audits. An internal audit will look at things like financial controls to make it harder for assets to be diverted from within the company. An external audit will declare that the firm's financial reports meet GAAP standards. Both are often conducted simultaneously.

Studies suggest that internal business fraud losses average 6% of revenue of all U.S. business revenue. A small percentage of owners make off with the most money, but employees are the most active. Since we have just learned about the materiality constraint, ask yourself if 6% of revenue is worth trying to recover. Yes, the cost/benefit constraint does kick in.

Position	Percent	Volume
Owner	12%	$1,000,000
Management	30%	$250,000
Employee	58%	$60,000

Table 2-2. Business fraud loss

A series of best practices have developed over time to control internal fraud. These internal controls cover the handling of cash and cash-generating items such as invoices and purchase orders, access to computer systems and programs, and preparation of financial statements.

The most common types of fraud committed by employees involve making charges to expense accounts to cover theft of cash/inventory, "lapping" (using a customer's check from one account to cover theft from a different account) and transaction fraud, deleting, altering, or adding false transactions to steal assets.

Fraud by owners and managers often takes place at man-

Tip-Offs to Fraud

Smart Managing

- **Financial pressures**—These are usually caused by an immediate financial need.
- **Poor internal controls**—These are especially crucial for the review and timely counting of liquid assets like cash.
- **Too much control**—The most common reason for the opportunity to commit financial crime is that too much authority or responsibility is placed in one employee, circumventing a good system of internal control.
- **Lax management**—Management must take responsibility for averting internal crime and properly supervise and review subordinates' work.
- **Failure to screen employees**—Integrity is tough to measure, so screen out those potential employees who have a known history of dishonesty.
- **Poor money management**—Employees with a known history of credit problems are at high risk for handling financial transactions. (See above.)
- **Personality changes**—These could be the result of financial pressures, marital problems, gambling, drugs, and alcohol—all of which can lead to theft.
- **Living beyond one's means**—Employee with conspicuous spending habits or a penchant for expensive items often support their lifestyles through internal crimes.
- **Outside business interests**—The financial obligations imposed by outside employee business interests provide a strong motivation for internal crimes.

---

agement levels above the one to which the internal control structure applies. Management fraud frequently involves using financial statements to create the illusion that the entity is healthier and more prosperous in order to cover misappropriation of assets. The misappropriation is usually shrouded in a maze of complex business transactions.

Internal controls include such procedures as monitoring activities, segregating financial responsibilities, physical control of cash and convertible assets, procedural controls for things like numbered invoices, access control to sensitive areas, and various authorization and approval levels.

> ### Control Your Controls
>
> Internal controls can sometimes make it very difficult to work efficiently—that cost/benefit constraint again. It once took me a month to get 16 signatures authorizing a $25,000 purchase of computers. That was when I worked for the government and they have since changed the procedure.

In establishing internal controls, good management decisions help in creating a positive work environment. If the controls are presented as prudent for the health of the company and designed to help protect employees from suspicion, acceptance is high. If the cost/benefit threshold is crossed and the controls restrict work and increase frustration, they often increase the possibility of fraud.

If your company has no internal controls or does not pay attention to them, it could be beneficial to have an audit with a stated objective of examining internal controls. After all, a main reason for internal controls is to reduce the risk to the integrity of the firm's financial statements.

Audits

There are three types of audits that CPAs perform—an audit, a compilation, and a review. Each comes with varying degrees of assurance. The assurance comes in the form of an auditor's letter. The wording in the letter is controlled as carefully as the moves in a kabuki dance. I just wish it were possible to talk about auditing without sounding like my mouth is full of peanut butter. Still, notice how many of the audit standards tie back into GAAP.

Selection of an auditor kicks off a chain of fairly standard procedures. The auditor and/or members of the audit team will interview key personnel through the various departments to learn about the current standing procedures. At this stage, they're just interested in how work is actually done.

In discussions with management, the auditor prepares an

Objectives and Scope Document, detailing the work to be performed. This document is presented to management. If management accepts, the auditors will proceed with the work in accordance with the objectives and parameters outlined. All this is in the planning phase.

The auditors will be looking at the control environment, information systems and communication, risk assessment, and the various control activities.

Control Environment

The control environment reflects the overall attitude, awareness, and actions of the board of directors, management, owners, and others concerning the importance of control and its profile in the entity. Seven areas collectively affect the control environment.

- Is integrity valued? What are the ethical values of the company? Is there a code of conduct? Do incentive and compensation programs support ethical behavior?
- Do the audit committee and board of directors oversee accounting policies and practices?
- What is the philosophy of management and operating style? Is there a constructive attitude toward financial reporting? Is there a responsible approach to risk?
- Is the assignment of authority and responsibility appropriately managed?
- Does the company show a commitment to competence? Does it have procedures for ensuring competence, requisite skills, and knowledge for particular jobs?
- Are the human resource policies and

> **How Many Can You Spot?**
>
> Look over the seven areas. Do you personally know of any situation in which you would have had to answer in the negative about a company? How many of these have you personally witnessed, either positive or negative? Now that you're learning some of the things auditors are supposed to look for, you'll be able to audit the auditors.

procedures adequate to provide sufficient, competent personnel with adequate resources?

- Is the organizational structure clear on who assigns and who accepts authority and responsibility?

Information and Communications

The information and communication part includes the accounting system. The accounting system, whether manual or computerized, is the methods and records set up to record, process, summarize, and report the firm's transactions. It must maintain accountability for all the related assets and liabilities.

- Can the system identify and record all valid transactions? This objective concerns the financial statement assertions of *existence* or *occurrence* and *completeness*.
- Does it describe on a timely basis the transactions in sufficient detail to permit proper classification of transactions for financial reporting? This objective concerns the financial statement assertion of *presentation* and *disclosure*.
- Can it measure the value of transactions in a manner that permits recording their proper monetary value in the financial statements? This objective concerns the financial statement assertion of *valuation* or *allocation*.
- Are transactions recorded in the proper accounting period? This objective concerns the financial statement assertions of *existence* or *occurrence* and *completeness*.
- Can it present the transactions and related disclosures in the financial statements? This objective concerns the financial statement assertions of *rights* and *obligations* and *presentation* and *disclosure*.

Communication means giving a clear understanding of each person's responsibilities for internal control. This would include reporting exceptions to an appropriate higher level within the entity. Communication takes such forms as policy manuals, accounting and financial reporting manuals, and memoranda.

Risk Assessment

Risk assessment aims to identify, assess, and manage risks that could affect the entity's ability to reach its major objectives. Once risks are identified, management considers the significance of the risks, the probabilities, and ways to manage them. Management may address specific risks or it may decide to accept a risk because of cost or other considerations. Risks can arise or change due to changes in regulatory or operating environment, personnel, or information systems; to rapid growth; and to new technology, lines of business, products, or activities.

Control Activities

Control activities are the policies and procedures that guide employees' actions to address risks and achieve management's objectives. Control activities include segregation of duties and controls on information processing.

Segregation of duties should create conditions where no one person is in a position to both perpetrate and conceal errors or irregularities in the normal course of processing information or data. This means procedures for separate custody, authorization, and recordkeeping.

In information processing, the auditor looks for general controls, application controls to check accuracy, completeness, authorization controls over transactions, and document controls.

Internal controls do have limits. Management can override them. If several employees collude, they can evade the controls. There are cost constraints as well. Finally, mistakes, including mistakes in judgment, can make a hash of controls.

In the fieldwork phase, auditors conduct interviews with people responsible for maintaining and preparing financial statements and operational reports. The auditors use various audit techniques to sample, test, and analyze the company's internal controls. Depending on company procedures, this could involve a paper chase using statistical methods to examine a number of transactions or a computer program that puts several test inputs through the system. The audit team gives frequent progress reports to management, keeping them abreast of preliminary findings.

When fieldwork is done, the audit team goes back to analyze its data and prepare its findings. After they are finished, the auditors make a formal presentation of their conclusions. What you hope for is a letter that says something along the lines of "We looked at these folks using all our good auditing tricks and we conclude that they are pretty good GAAPers." If there are deviations from GAAP that you agree to change, the audit may mention that they found deviations, but that management is taking corrective action.

What you don't want is to get into a situation where the auditor sees a discrepancy and brings it to your attention and you disagree that it's a problem and refuse to do anything about it. Then the auditor will give you a letter finding "material breach" and your stock will tank and the bank will call the loan.

Work with the auditors. They're really trying to help you. If the auditors find a few things, they may come back in a year or so to see how you're doing at making the recommended changes.

Manager's Checklist for Chapter 2

❑ GAAP developed to help small investors have confidence in financial statements so that they would be encouraged to invest. Thus, GAAP is the foundation for all financial statements.

❑ GAAP can be inconsistent in both logic and application. Considerable judgment is often needed to reach a compatible decision.

❑ Auditing is a way to assess how well GAAP has been implemented.

❑ GAAP values an ethical stance to business activities.

❑ No internal controls are safe against fraud and collusion.

Financial Statements

The Lemonade Stand

It's a hot August afternoon. Dick and Jane open their lemonade stand to catch the coming home from work trade. They get Molly and Tom to mix the lemonade, serve drinks, and collect cash while they drum up customers. Molly's older brother, James, is in charge of getting the lemonade supplies and helping things go smoothly. Another day of basic business.

In any business, owners provide the funds. Managers buy equipment, inventory, and other assets. Managers, in conjunction with owners, develop plans and set goals. Those goals include making a profit. The owners and managers may also decide they want to sell a quality product at a high profit, donate a percentage of profits, and/or research new technology.

As the business operates, revenue comes in from the sale of goods. The goods cost money, so some profits go to buy more goods and the equipment to run the business. Profits also pay the managers for their effort and reward the owners for the risk they took.

As the lemonade stand grows, it may need more help from the outside world to thrive. It needs to borrow money for working capital to manage its cash flow and meet its obligations. If the managers weren't preparing financial statements before to track progress and identify weak points, they must now. They have to communicate to the outside world. To help show good faith to creditors, they might have external auditors review financial statements. Now, a wide variety of users access the various statements to help them make their decisions. When the lemonade stand grows into a nationwide franchise, the financial statements will be enshrined in a glossy annual report complete with a statement from the president, a management letter, and other trappings of success.

They are still just financial statements showing the gozinta and gozouta. There are just more accounts, more options, and

---

CAUTION!

What Type of Lemonade Stand Are You?

This is an important question. The structure of Dick and Jane's lemonade stand makes only a small difference in the type of financial statements they must prepare, but a large difference in their legal and tax position.

There are three main types of business organizations in the U.S.: sole proprietors, partnerships, and corporations. The sole proprietor is one person operating a business. There may be employees, but the proprietor will report revenues, expenses, and income on his or her personal tax return. The structure and accounting activities are largely tax-driven.

Partnerships—and there are different flavors—are two or more people conducting a business. Certain operational expenses can be deducted through the partnership. Income flows through to the individual partners based on their agreement. Professionals—accountants, architects, doctors, and lawyers—commonly form partnerships.

Corporations are distinct legal individuals. A corporation reports and pays taxes as required before distributing profit to owners. Several corporate entities combine features of all three. S corporations and limited liability companies (LLC) are two currently popular choices.

The choice of entity, like the choice of accounting system, can have an impact on your tax, legal, and accounting requirements.

more footnotes explaining the arcane ins and outs of accounting. As complicated as these things can get, it's important to remember that the basic business is still there.

Load, Wash, Rinse, Spin, Dry

Financial statements are a chief end product of sequential steps generally called the *accounting cycle.* The accounting cycle details a series of repeated procedures on different kinds of data. This stable repetition helps meet the calls for reliability, relevance, and consistency, to tick off just a few of the GAAP mandates.

We've already met most of the elements of the accounting transaction cycle. The cycle outlines the steps to be followed for receiving, entering, and presenting the transaction data that comes into the firm. The cycle ends with preparing for the next cycle. While different authors may assign different names and condense or expand certain areas, the accounting cycle will include the following steps:

1. Analyze business transactions.
2. Journalize transactions.
3. Post transactions to the ledger accounts.
4. Prepare a trial balance of the general ledger.
5. Analyze, prepare, and post the adjusting entries.
6. Prepare an adjusted trial balance.
7. Prepare the financial statements: income statement, balance sheet, and statement of cash flows.
8. Journalize and post the closing entries.
9. Prepare a post-closing trial balance.

We learned in Chapter 1 there would be a flow of gozintas and gozoutas that we would visualize and fit into the accounting equation, or its corollary, the revenue proposition. Once the transaction is analyzed, the whole is recorded in the general journal. Then, the accounting system, either a computer or a Cratchit, groups each relevant piece of that transaction into individual account ledgers. These individual ledgers are then summed in the general ledger.

The process has been to record the compound elements of the transaction in the general journal. That entry is then broken down into account elements, like separating whites and colors, to push the laundry metaphor. Getting to the general ledger requires a first test of the accounting equation. All the accounts that normally carry a debit balance are summed against all the accounts that normally carry a credit balance. Remember from Chapter 1 that showed how assets normally carry a debit balance and liabilities/equities have a credit balance? Are the results in balance?

In a manual environment, the trial balance is often not in balance. Then, the problems must be exposed. Adjusting entries generally are made to meet the requirements of accrual accounting. The revenues are recorded when earned and expenses reported when incurred. We test the accounting equation again. There'll be more on adjusting entries later. Look on this as the rinse phase.

When the adjusted trial balance is in balance, it's used to prepare the financial statement(s). This might be considered the spin cycle. Then, any entries needed to close out this period and prepare for the next are posted. Closing involves zeroing out the revenue and expense accounts, while leaving the asset, liability, and equity accounts intact. A final balancing vindication of the accounting equation confirms that we're set to face the next cycle in getting and spending.

Smart Managing

Be a RYPR (Repetition Yields Positive Results)

Oh, this sounds so tedious and painstaking. Is it all really necessary? Yes. You've no doubt discovered that most people—be they owners, managers, employees, customers, vendors, or the tax collector—get a bit persnickety when it comes down to money. These procedures, developed, tested, and proven over time, will guide you through many financial rapids.

Computers have taken over much of the mind porridge chores in accounting. Still, the underlying concepts of GAAP must be understood to make the most effective use of the analysis tools. Whether it's putting a bat on a ball, practicing an aria, or polishing a sales call, repetition yields positive results.

Past as Prologue

Financial statements are historical documents. They report the past. Since there's no way to directly know the future, we use financial statements—past performance—to forecast the future. If the accounting system operates under GAAP and the financial statements are prepared according to GAAP, we can use a variety of forecasting and analysis tools to predict the future performance of the business. This approach has many flaws, but it's the most reliable of a shaky lot. (Shamans reading chicken guts and monkeys throwing darts are two discarded forecasting tools, although the monkeys still have a few adherents.)

From recording information in the general journal through the accounting cycle, the raw accounting information has three main purposes—financial data for external users and management, management cost results to guide decision making, and tax information for governmental authorities. Management can prepare several reports from this data. For present purposes, we will focus on three reports: the balance sheet, the income statement, and the statement of cash flows. Each of these statements highlights a particular portion of the accounting equation and its corollaries, to help you determine meaningful things about the activity of the enterprise. Recall the three questions posed at the start of this book. How much money came in? Where did the money go? How much money is left?

The income statement answers the first question. The revenue and expense accounts are added up for a given period of time, typically a year. The statement of cash flows solves the second question. It tracks where cash came from what it was used for. It also tracks activity for a given time period. Finally, the balance sheet polishes off the third of the three questions. It shows what's left in the company. It's the only one that uses a point in time, typically the end of the fiscal year.

All the gozinta and gozouta transactions of the business can be assigned to one of three categories of activities—operating, investing, and financing. Operating activities are what make the profits for the enterprise. Investing activities support operations through buying and selling the long-term assets needed to carry out operations. Those assets are paid for through the financing activities that come up with the cash and repay borrowed money.

Financial Statements	Business Activities

Income Statement
  Revenues
  Expenses
	Operating Activities

Statement of Cash Flows
  Operating Activities
  Investing Activities
  Financing Activities
	Operating Activities
	Investing Activities
	Financing Activities

Balance Sheet
  Current Assets
  Long-Term Assets
  Current Liabilities
  Long-Term Liabilities
  Equity
	Operating Activities
	Investing Activities
	Operating Activities
	Financing Activities
	Financing Activities

Table 3-1. Financial statements and categories of activities

As we step through the financial statements, we can see where each category of activity fits.

The Income Statement

The generic income statement below contains most of the elements found in a comprehensive income statement for a corporation. There's certainly enough flexibility in the format to permit additions and subtractions based on the need to communicate business activity. In Chapter 1, we took a simplified approach to the income statement. The full income statement formula is an expanded accounting equation.

assets = liabilities + equity + revenues − expenses + gains − losses

Solving algebraically and then reducing it to the normal balance of each account yields the following:

assets + expenses + losses = liabilities + equity +
revenue + gain or debits = credits

The income statement (Table 3-2) shows the profitability of the company.

The income statement is formatted with combinations of bold highlighting, indentation, preliminary account sums, and

Income Statement
General Widget, Inc.
December 31, 200_

Account Names	Account Sums	Aggregated Sums and Totals
Sales Revenue		3,500,000
Cost of Sales		
Materials	575,000	
Labor	825,000	
Overhead	350,000	1,750,000
Gross Margin		1,750,000
Operating Expense		
Selling	750,000	
General and		
Administrative	650,000	
Depreciation and		
Amortization	100,000	1,500,000
Operating Income		250,000
Other Income and Expenses		
Dividends and Interest	25,000	
Interest Expense	(75,000)	
Unusual/Extraordinary Items	150,000	100,000
Income Before Tax		350,000
Income Tax (t = .34)		119,000
Net Income		231,000

Table 3-2. Income statement

aggregated category sums so the information is presented as clearly as possible. One of the few constants is that it will always show the company name, the type of statement, and the period being reported.

In this example, perhaps a small set design company, the Sales Revenue, the top line, is the money received from customers for the product. There are direct manufacturing costs involved and company records expenses for the raw material, the labor of the people who build the sets, and the overhead associated with manufacture. This overhead might be the shop where construction takes place as well as utility, insurance, and other costs associated with the defined work. Subtract these costs from Revenue to yield the Gross Margin.

Since this income statement calculates a Cost of Sales, General Widget (GW) provides a product. If GW were a service company, these costs would not appear. There are

---

Key Term

Revenue Cash coming into the business as a result of operations.

Materials Raw materials used in a manufacturing or production process.

Labor Labor resources used in the manufacturing or production process.

Overhead All costs related to manufacturing or production process, including plant, equipment, supplies, depreciation, and utilities.

Selling Costs related to sales operations.

General and Administrative Costs incurred by the company other than production or sales, including staff, staff equipment, and staff supplies.

Operating Income Income after subtracting the costs of production and operation.

Dividends and Interest Income from investments unrelated to business operations.

Interest Expense Interest paid on bank loans and other debt.

Unusual/Extraordinary Gains or losses associated with nonroutine events, such as selling an asset or an operation, receiving a large settlement, or natural disaster damage.

variations in the income statement format depending on industry, company size, and disclosure needs. They will still follow the general sequence resolving debits and credits. Note also that this example classifies the income as it related first to production, the Gross Margin, also called "income from continuing operations." Many consider this number the most important predictor of future business health. If it's high, your business generates enough cash to support the activity that's actually making money.

From the Gross Margin, subtract all the expenses incurred in "keeping the doors open" to yield Operating Income. This subdivision of the income statement is not a GAAP requirement, but it gives an idea of the strength and profitability of the core business operation. Then both expenses and income not related to operations are calculated. Often these are single-event items that will not recur—the tornado that took the roof or the obscure patent sold for big bucks. That brings us to Income Before Tax. We subtract the income tax and finally reach the bottom line, Net Income. This is how much we made. To know how well GW did as a company, you would have to compare this 7% return with others in the widget industry. It could be great, fair, or downright anemic.

Statement of Cash Flows

For many years, the accounting profession worked to get a grip on how to report the information contained in the statement of cash flows. In the 1960s, a funds statement was developed to meet the need for public companies to report this information. It languished from lack of attention. It wasn't until late 1987 that the Accounting Principles Board established the format for the statement of cash flows.

I had a business school professor who liked to claim, "No one went broke making a profit." Well, the statement of cash flows shows you how it can be done. If your collections don't keep up with your payment obligations, you'll run out of cash and be forced into bankruptcy. All those accounts receivable propping up the balance sheet lose cash value if they can't be

Know Your Audience

Who are the customers for these financial statements and what uses will they make of them? That's a very broad question. Managers use them internally to gauge and guide management decisions. Interested external parties could include the following:

- Current or potential investors evaluating the firm's prospects
- Creditors deciding whether or not to lend money
- Investment advisors and economists forecasting the future prospects for the company or the industry
- Customers evaluating you for your ability to complete long-term assignments
- Tax authorities monitoring compliance
- News media reporting on business and the economy
- Competitors wanting to know your strategies

Public financial statements generate a lot of interest and scrutiny. People invest a lot of time and treasure in the results. Is there any wonder people get upset when they get bogus information?

collected. Creditors prefer steak to paper, but will take potatoes if that's all you have left.

The information in the income statement and the balance sheet comes from end-state accounts. The statement of cash flows (Table 3-3) is the only report that uses "flow" information. Changes in the cash flow can often explain why balance sheet accounts changed. The statement is also useful in projecting the liquidity of a business over time. One clear thing it will show is how a business uses the profits that it generates.

The first section of the statement is for *operating* activities. Operating activities are those things that generate cash income. These include sales receipts as well as inventory or manufacturer purchase. Cash from operations can be negative, and often is, especially in growing companies. At the start, operating losses rise as cash is spent for expenses. As you add business, you start to book some revenue. A lot of that revenue is in the form of accounts receivable, so your cash collection rate is a bit slow. Not for nothing is it called *cash burn*. Without loans or personal capital coming in to feed the fire, a company can be reduced to cinders.

A lot of that cash is going to *investing* activities. Investments are the power tools, shop buildings, and office equipment needed to get things started. It doesn't matter if you are buying them outright or financing them, you'll have to account for them. How you chose to pay for your assets will affect your cash flow. Which path you choose will depend on several variables—amount, interest rate, expected payback time, and forecast of future cash flows.

If you chose to use debt financing, the *financing* activities section is where you'll record the loan proceeds. This section also shows the gozintas and gozoutas of cash to the owners through stock purchases, dividend payments, or shareholder loans.

Many companies are woefully undercapitalized, sometimes by owner intent, often through ignorance of the need. To be competitive, business owners and managers must continually plan to keep the cash flowing into the company. The U. S. Small Business Administration names ineffective cash flow management as one of the top reasons why firms fail.

There are two methods used to present statement of cash flows information, the *indirect* method (as in Table 3-3) and the *direct* method. The methods are different in their treatment of operating activities only. Most companies use the indirect method, because it's easier. Most banks prefer the direct method, as it provides more information.

The indirect method does not report the operating cash flows. Instead, the operating activities section reconciles net income and net operating cash flows. You start with the net income from your income statement. You then adjust this accrual amount for items that do not affect cash flows. There are three basic types of adjustments in the operating activities section. The first involves non-cash outlays, such as depreciation or amortization. Then, adjust for gains and loses on transactions reported in other sections of the statement of cash flows. Finally, convert all current operating assets and liabilities from the accrual to the cash basis.

General Widget, Inc.
Statement of Cash Flows
For the Year Ended December 31, 200_

Indirect Method	
Operating Activities	
Sales Receipts	3,500,000
Payments for Products	(1,750,000)
Payments for Operations	(1,500,000)
Payments for Interest	(75,000)
Payments for Taxes	(119,000
Unusual Items	150,000
Net Cash (Used) by	
Operating Activities	206,000
Investing Activities	
Purchase of Property, Plant,	
and Equipment	(1,850,000
Sales of Property, Plant, and	
Equipment	
Interest and Dividend Income	75,000
Net Cash (Used) by Investing	
Activities	(1,775,000)
Financing Activities	
Short-Term Debt	580,000
Long-Term Debt	1,000,000
Capital Stock Issued	450,000
Cash Dividends	
Net Cash (Used) by Financing	
Activities	2,030,000
Net (Decrease) in Cash	461,000
Cash at Beginning of Year	(111,000)
Cash at End of Year	350,000

Table 3-3. Statement of cash flows

A way to visualize the cash coming in is with a corollary of the accounting equation (Table 3-4).

In the direct method, the net cash flow from operations is computed directly as the net sum of the operating cash flows. Your firm will do one or the other. Ask about why the particular

	Cash +	Other Assets =	Liabilities +	Equity
Collect accounts receivable	Increase	Decrease		
Borrow money or accounts payable	Increase		Increase	
Sell shares, add capital	Increase			Increase
Repay debt	Decrease		Decrease	
Loss on net income	Decrease			Decrease
Pay shareholder dividend	Decrease			Decrease

Table 3-4. Accounting equation

statement form was chosen and just learn it.

The Balance Sheet

The balance sheet is the accounting equation. It lists the firm's assets, liabilities, and equity as of a specific date. In this respect it's a position statement rather than flow statement. The balance sheet is the company's solvency report card. Typically, the date is the end of the firm's reporting fiscal year. However, computer software has made generating reports vastly easier. It's not uncommon for a manager to run off last night's balance sheet to read with coffee in the morning.

The balance sheet always balances because of the double-entry system and debit-credit recording rule correctly applied. Each asset increase in the equation must have one or more of the following:

- asset decrease
- liability increase
- equity increase
- revenue increase
- gain increase
- expense decrease
- loss decrease

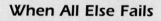

When All Else Fails

When faced with a recalcitrant balance sheet, assuming one side proves correct, look in the opposite accounts. If all else fails and the amount out of balance is small relative to your sales, you can always set up a *cash over/short* account to balance. While it's not recommended, remember the GAAP cost/benefit quality of information and the materiality constraint. If there's no financial impact in the adjustment, it's acceptable.

It's all contained algebraically within the equation. There are no other options. Recall that the balance sheets for Enron and WorldCom were mathematically correct.

The balance sheet reports the resources and obligations of the firm. Because it's a mixture of many different assets and liabilities with varying cost structures, it can be a bit confusing. Remember the consistency aspect of GAAP quality? That's the one that said land bought for $100,000 20 years ago is still carried on the books at $100,000, even though it may be worth $10,000,000. Similarly, that new $1,000,000 machine that you bought a year ago may have been overtaken by such superior technology

Key Term

Accounts receivable Money due from customers for goods and services.

Marketable securities Stocks, bonds, or other financial instrument held by the company.

Inventory Goods available for sale.

Property, plant, and equipment The buildings and machinery; the fixed assets of the company.

Accounts payable Money the company owes to vendors for good or services rendered.

Notes payable A loan or obligation to be paid, current portion of a long-term debt.

Income taxes payable Taxes due in the current year.

Accrued expenses Expenses that will be due but have not yet been paid.

Deferred income taxes An estimate of the taxes that would be due if assets were sold at stated value.

Paid-in capital Total amount of cash and other assets paid in to the corporation by stockholders in exchange for capital stock.

Retained earnings All the money a company has earned since start-up minus dividends, a record of money the company has put back into the business.

Stockholders' equity The amount of financing provided by owners of the business and operations.

that you can't even give it away. Still, it's on the books for $1,000,000, less accumulated depreciation.

There are some other accounts that have some inherent risk. The accounts receivable may not all collect. If the inventory is particularly high, that could be a sign that the product is not moving. The balance sheet consists of many accounts that are actually estimates that may or may not come true. Understanding the potential limitations helps when considering the balance sheet in conjunction with other financial statements (see Figure 3-5).

A Delicate Balance: The Adjusting Entries

The GAAP revenue recognition and matching principles require that the revenue from a particular accounting period be

Know What You're Signing

Some asset accounts, used in daily operations, help to generate revenue. These assets, bought in one accounting period, are either not used or not completely used by the end of the accounting period. The revenue coming from those assets should be reconciled. Managers are often asked to sign and take responsibility for the truth of financial statements.

If you have to sign adjusting entries, determine the rationale for the treatment and the impact it will have on the financial statements. This particular area of matching revenue and expenses to the correct accounting period has been subject to abuse. It now draws more scrutiny. Managers should understand the GAAP principles behind adjusting entries and how they are entered.

General Widget, Inc.
Balance Sheet
December 31, 200_

Assets	
Current Assets	
Cash	350,000
Accounts Receivable	500,000
Marketable Securities	68,000
Inventory	444,400
Prepaid Expenses	15,000
Total Current Assets	1,377,400
Property, Plant, Equipment	
Land	600,000
Buildings	1,100,000
Machinery	1,390,000
Furniture and Fixtures	300,000
Vehicles	315,000
Accumulated Depreciation	95,000
Net Property, Plant, Equipment	3,800,000
Total Assets	5,177,400

Liabilities	
Current Liabilities	
Accounts Payable	580,000
Notes Payable	199,000
Accrued Expenses	95,000
Income Taxes Payable	43,400
Total Current Liabilities	917,400
Long-Term Liabilities	
Deferred Taxes	350,000
Long-Term Debt	2,000,000
Total Liabilities	3,267,400

Table 3-5. Balance sheet (continued on next page)

matched with expenses that help cause that revenue. That way, external users will have a more accurate picture of profitability.

The accrual accounting setup provides for accounts to carry amounts into the future and then peel off as they enter the applicable period.

Shareholder Equity	
Preferred Stock	200,000
Common Stock	1,190,000
Paid-in Capital	420,000
Retained Earnings	100,000
Total Equity	1,910,000
Total Liabilities and Shareholder Equity	5,177,400

Figure 3-5. Balance sheet (continued)

Let's look at the simple example of paying the insurance bill. The annual bill is $7,200 if paid in advance, $8,400 in two equal installments, or $800 on a monthly basis. Being prudent managers, we take the time value of money into account. We pay the $7,200 in June to cover the insurance bill for the entire 12 months. Our fiscal year ends December 31, so we'll have to carry the insurance over.

When we've paid for the insurance, it's an asset. When the month comes around, the portion of the asset covering the month converts to an expense. On the books, it will look like Table 3-6.

By the end of the year, the accumulated accounts will show the ledger entries in Table 3-7.

You can set some accounting systems do this automatically. With others, you have to remember to post the transaction monthly. At the start of the next year, the balance in the asset account must be carried forward while the expense account is cleared (Table 3-8).

Common adjusting entries involve carrying over payroll-related data to the next accounting period. Thus, employee wages and taxes earned in the last period but not payable until the new period, along with the associated employer share of FICA and other taxes due, need an adjusting entry. Other adjustments include the need to accrue revenues and expenses related to interest, depreciation, inventory changes, dividends, or income tax payable. Finally, if your day-to-day books are

General Ledger

Date	Account	Ref	Debit	Credit
June 1	Prepaid insurance		$7,200	
	Cash			$7,200
	Annual insurance bill			

Ledger Account

Date	Account	Ref	Debit	Credit	Balance
June 1	Prepaid insurance		$7,200		$7,200
June 30	Prepaid insurance			$600	$6,600

Ledger Account

Date	Account	Ref	Debit	Credit	Balance
June 30	Insurance expense		$600		$600

Table 3-6. Insurance: general journal and ledger accounts

Ledger Account

Date	Account	Ref	Debit	Credit	Balance
Dec 31	Prepaid insurance				$3,600
Dec 31				$600	$3,000

Ledger Account

Date	Account	Ref	Debit	Credit	Balance
Dec 31	Insurance expense				$3,600
Dec 31			$600		$4,200

Table 3-7. Insurance: ledger accounts

maintained on a cash basis, set up an accounts receivable and accounts payable balance.

Ledger Account

Date	Account	Ref	Debit	Credit	Balance
Jan 1	Prepaid insurance				$3,000
Jan 31				$600	$2,400

Ledger Account

Date	Account	Ref	Debit	Credit	Balance
Dec 31	Insurance expense				
Dec 31			$600		$600

Table 3-8. Insurance: ledger accounts

Manager's Checklist for Chapter 3

❏ There are many forms for business entities. These forms principally relate to legal and tax concerns, although each has slightly different accounting requirements.

❏ The accounting cycle outlines a series of steps that should be followed to conform to GAAP. These procedures aim to reduce errors and improve the accuracy of financial statements.

❏ Financial statements are historical documents useful to many groups of users, both internal and external to the company. The financial statements help show the profitability and solvency of the company.

❏ The income statement shows how much money the company made.

❏ The statement of cash flows shows how the company used the money it made.

❏ The balance sheet shows how much is left of what the company made.

❏ Adjusting statements clarify and account for transactions that span accounting periods.

Financial Ratios

Faced with the columns and rows of numbers in financial statements, a manager could become discouraged at the task of wresting meaning from such material. Outside of the readily apparent "top line" and "bottom line," what information can be gained from financial statements? Worlds. The information in a balance sheet and an income statement can give your management activities structure, direction, and meaning.

What Measures Performance?

What are your personal job performance standards? What are the goals you set for yourself each day, each month, each year? How do you keep score? How does your organization measure accomplishment? What goals does the organization expect you to meet?

If you're in a larger company, chances are there's a formal management program, something like Total Quality Management (TQM) or Six Sigma. If you're with a smaller firm or partnership, you might use something like gross sales as a target. You might also want to use something like financial ratio analysis.

Even the structured management programs have financial analysis at their heart. Those programs just pack a few more variables into the equation and try to set a finer sieve. The resulting financial performance analysis is the language of goals, objectives, and results. A ratio is a number that expresses a mathematical relationship between two quantities, such as items on balance sheets and income statements. Financial ratio concepts are important for managing cash, capital investment, profitability, and risk. They're the primary way to speak with depth and precision about management job performance and achieving enterprise goals.

Because a ratio is a mathematical operation, it can be categorized within broad subject groupings. Many combinations can be tested and the results proved. Ratio analysis has developed into four main analysis areas: *liquidity*, *debt*, *activity*, and *profitability*.

Financial ratio analysis lets you calculate and compare relationships derived from information in the financial statements. The current interaction and historic trends of these ratios can be used to make inferences about a company's financial condition, its operations, and its attractiveness as an investment or credit risk.

> **Key Term**
>
> **Ratio** A number that expresses a mathematical relationship between two quantities. For example, the ratio of 1,000 to 500 is 2:1 or 2. In financial terms, a ratio can show relationships between various items appearing on balance sheets and income statements and other items.
>
> The same ratio may travel under several names. This can cause confusion. Look for the accounts being used as the numerator and denominator and you may know the ratio under a different name. In addition, a derived ratio can become part of another ratio calculation.

A ratio draws meaning through comparison with other data and standards. By itself, a financial ratio is not worth much. In context, a manager or outside analyst can tease out meaning to develop an understanding of a company's situation and developing trends.

Here's an example. Gross profit margin (GPM) is a ratio, the gross or total profit from operations divided by the total sales or revenues of a company, expressed as a percentage. Let's say that the gross profit margin was 17%. Out of context, 17% means nothing. If we could find out the GPM for similar companies of similar size in similar markets, then we could say something meaningful. If we learn that this company's competitors have GPMs of 10%, we know that the company is almost twice as profitable as its industry peers. By any standard, that's quite good. If we also know that the historical trend is up, that GPM has been rising steadily for the last few years, this would also be a favorable sign. We could conclude that management has in place valuable business policies and strategies. In this

Finding Industry Ratios

TRICKS OF THE TRADE

Industry ratios are classified by either SIC or NAICS codes. The U.S. government developed these systems in order to provide a standard method for collecting and analyzing economic information.

The older SIC (Standard Industrial Classification) system classifies companies and industries by their primary line of business. The North American Industrial Classification System (NAICS), which provides codes for over 350 new industries, is gradually replacing the SIC system. So, you may find some sources that use SIC, while others will use NAICS.

Use the following sources to identify SIC and NAICS codes for an industry:
* *Standard Industrial Classification (SIC) Manual*
* *North American Industry Classification System—United States*
* 1997 NAICS and 1987 SIC Correspondence Tables

Match SIC codes with NAICS codes or match NAICS codes with SIC codes.

Several commercial vendors collect and collate financial ratio information. Two of them are Dun and Bradstreet and The Risk Management Association (formerly Robert Morris Associates).

See the Resources section in the back for additional information.

case, we would better understand and appreciate the financial status of the company.

That's only one example of the information to be acquired through financial ratio analysis. There's a ratio for almost any question you'd care to ask—and a couple you might not dare. The ratio formulas are valuable for the questions they answer. In some cases, they're more valuable because of the additional questions they raise. To bring some order to these multiple ratios, they're grouped into categories that tell us about different parts of a company's finances and operations. Here is an overview of some of the ratio categories.

Liquidity ratios give a picture of a company's short-term financial solvency. You may consider them an immediate "going concern" test. If these numbers are bad, the company may not be able to meet next week's payroll.

Activity ratios use turnover measures to show how efficiently a company operates and uses its assets. Activity ratios are often called *operational ratios*.

Debt ratios show the extent that debt is used in a company's capital structure. They are also often called *leverage ratios*.

Profitability ratios use various profit margin analyses to show return on sales and capital.

Ratios also allow quick comparisons between your business and other businesses in your industry. Banks and investors use

Liquidity ratios Ratios that measure a company's ability to pay its short-term debts on time, its short-term financial solvency. Also known as *solvency ratios*.

Activity ratios Ratios that show how efficiently a company operates and uses its assets. Also known as *operational ratios*.

Debt ratios Ratios that show to what extent and how well a company uses borrowed funds to finance its operations. Also known as *leverage ratios*.

Profitability ratios Ratios that use various profit margin analyses to show return on sales and capital, as a measure of how well a company is using its resources to generate profits.

them to help decide whether a business is a good credit or investment risk. Managers look at ratios to monitor operations and spot weak areas and inefficiency. For example, ratios can indicate whether a business is carrying a dangerous amount of debt, holding too much inventory, or not collecting accounts receivable quickly enough. Managers could also look at their customers' and vendors' ratios to assess any risk involved.

One key to using ratios is finding a baseline, a point of comparison. Usually, you would be comparing your firm's ratios with the average for your industry or with your own ratios for the same period in a previous year.

Your CPA, a financial advisor, or a staff person should be able to help you calculate these ratios as they relate to your financial statements. Their initial input may be able to help you determine whether or not the ratios are in line for your business and industry. After you become familiar with ratio analysis, checking these numbers should become a steady habit, like checking the weather forecast to decide what clothes to wear. We'll also give you a chance to practice below.

Not all of the ratios matter to everybody, of course. Credit analysts, those persons interpreting the financial ratios from the lender's perspective, focus on the "downside" risk. Since their revenue comes from interest earned, they gain none of the upside from an improvement in operations and increased prof-

GIGO

Context is everything in ratio analysis. Like computer programming, ratio analysis follows the law of GIGO—*"garbage in, garbage out."* Comparing leverage ratios between a California electric company and an Ohio water company lacks utility, even though both are utilities. Examining the profitability ratios of a cyclical company over less than a full business cycle would fail to give an accurate long-term measure of profitability. Historical data, in the face of deep changes in a company's state or prospects, would predict little about future trends. If, for example, the company has merged with another or made a major change in its technology, its historical ratios would tell little about its future prospects.

its. They pay great mind to liquidity and debt ratios to determine a company's financial risk. Equity stock analysts look more to the activity and profitability ratios to determine the future profits that could pass to the shareholder.

Although financial ratio analysis is well developed and the actual ratios are well known, practicing financial analysts often build up their own measures for particular industries and even individual companies. Analysts will often differ drastically in their conclusions from the same ratio analysis. It's an art as well as a science.

Liquidity Ratios

Liquidity ratios (or *solvency ratios*) include the current ratio, the quick ratio, and net working capital.

Current Ratio

This is the standard measure of any business's financial health. The current ratio measures the ability of the firm to pay its current bills. You derive this ratio from the figures on your balance sheet. It tells whether a company has enough assets to cover its liabilities.

$$\text{current ratio} = \frac{\text{current assets}}{\text{current liabilities}}$$

Current assets include cash, accounts receivable, marketable securities, inventory, and any prepaid expenses like insurance or taxes. Current liabilities include accounts payable, current interest due on long-term debt, like taxes payable and salaries payable.

Generally, the higher the current ratio, the greater the safety margin between current obligations and the ability to pay them. The benchmark current ratio is 2:1.

Quick Ratio: "Acid Test"

The quick ratio is similar to the current ratio, but it's a tougher measure of liquidity than the current ratio, because it excludes inventories. Inventories typically take time to convert to ready cash. Thus, most analysts find them illiquid, not a cash equivalent.

(There's some question about how the "acid test" derived its name. Majority opinion holds it stems from the practice of proving precious metals through chemical analysis. Others, more fanciful, say it grew from the practice of discouraging defaulters by throwing acid on them.)

$$\text{quick ratio} = \frac{(\text{current assets} - \text{inventory})}{\text{current liabilities}}$$

Generally, the quick ratio should be lower than the current ratio, because the inventory figure drops from the calculation. A higher ratio correlates to a higher level of liquidity. This usually corresponds to better financial health. The quick ratio also indicates whether a business could pay off its debts quickly, if necessary. The desired quick ratio is at least 1:1. A lower ratio flags questions about whether the firm can continue to meet its outstanding obligations.

Net Working Capital (NWC)

Net working capital is not really a ratio in the strictest sense; it's just a number. You simply subtract the balance sheet current liabilities from the current assets. The result shows how much cash you have to work with. If the number is negative, plan to correct that situation as soon as possible. You should develop a notion of just what your NWC needs are. Many businesses set up NWC credit lines to make sure they don't run out of cash at a critical point.

$$\text{net working capital} = \text{current assets} - \text{current liabilities}$$

Note that NWC is included here because this figure is used in compound ratio calculations.

Activity Ratios

Activity ratios measure how well a company conducts its business operations. Activity ratios include the average collection period, the average payment period, the fixed assets turnover ratio, the total assets turnover ratio, and the inventory turnover ratio.

Average Collection Period (ACP)

This ratio, also known as *days sales outstanding,* shows how quickly a company converts accounts receivable into cash. A lower ratio is better: the lower the figure, the faster the company converts. This shows that the company is not giving out interest-free loans to customers for long periods of time. A low ACP also reduces the risk of default.

$$\text{average collection period} = \frac{\text{accounts receivable}}{(\text{sales} / 360 \text{ days})}$$

Accounts receivable count all customer credit obligations. Certain businesses that have a substantial amount of installment loans or notes may include the short-term (less than one year) amounts due. The sales figure includes sales for the prior four quarters. You may also calculate the figure on a quarterly basis. In that case, use 90 instead of 360 days. The accounts collection period varies from industry to industry, but in all cases, the shorter the better.

Average Payment Period (APP)

This ratio, also known as the *accounts payable turnover* ratio, tells how quickly a company is paying its bills, how often its payables turn over during the year.

$$\text{average payment period} = \frac{\text{accounts payable}}{(\text{purchases} / 360 \text{ days})}$$

A high ratio means a relatively short time between purchase of goods and services and payment for them; that is, the company pays its bills on time. A low ratio may be a sign that the company has chronic cash shortages. It could also mean that it delays paying bills to wring the maximum benefit possible from its cash. This ratio varies from industry to industry. Comparisons will be within your own industry.

Fixed Assets Turnover (FAT) Ratio

This ratio measures how efficiently a company uses its fixed assets to generate sales: the higher the better. From the balance sheet, take the sum of all property, plant, and equipment and

Encourage Collections

TRICKS OF THE TRADE Many companies want a low ACP and a high APP. Because of the time value of money, the quicker you can collect cash and longer you hold off paying for your purchases, the more you can leverage your resources to your own economic benefit. Companies can invest in short-term financial markets where they can earn a few dollars in interest even overnight. If your company is large, managing cash efficiently, like managing any other asset well, can return a significant chunk of change.

To encourage prompt payment, many companies offer discounts. One standard offer is a 2% discount if the bill is paid in 10 days, rather than the usual 30 days. This is shown on the bill as "2/10 net 30." Many companies will also charge and enforce interest penalties on late payments. A clear, well-managed collections policy encourages a low ACP. Doing business with vendors with lax payment policies could lead to a high ACP on your end and an even higher APP.

divide that number into gross sales from the income statement.

$$\text{fixed assets turnover} = \frac{\text{sales}}{\text{fixed assets}}$$

The fixed assets turnover result shows the relationship between $1 in fixed assets and of $1 sales. A low FAT ratio may mean that management is actually porking out on perks. Assets are going for fancy buildings and the latest computer gadgets rather than making their way back to the bottom line. Different industries have different benchmarks.

Total Assets Turnover (TAT) Ratio

This ratio measures how well a company generates sales from assets. It's similar to the fixed assets turnover but includes all assets—current, fixed, other long-term. A high ratio here shows that sales, the numerator, is substantially higher than the denominator. It means you're managing your assets well.

$$\text{total asset turnover} = \frac{\text{sales}}{\text{total assets}}$$

The total assets turnover result is industry-dependent.

Inventory Turnover (IT) Ratio

The inventory turnover ratio shows how often a company replaces its inventory. This is a key management performance indicator for retail businesses. The more times the inventory is sold and replaced during the year, the more likely the company is to be successful. The turnover is meaningful only when comparing with other firms in the industry or a company's prior turnover ratios. In some industries the average is one or two turns per year while in others it's 10, 20, or more. Compare the turnovers of an aircraft dealership and an ice cream shop.

$$\text{inventory turnover} = \frac{\text{cost of goods sold}}{\text{total inventory}}$$

This calculation uses the cost of goods sold figure as the numerator, since inventories are usually carried at cost. The formula can also use total sales as the numerator; however, this can be an inaccurate test of financial performance to determine the inventory turnover rate.

A high inventory turnover ratio shows that a company can sustain sales volume. Because inventories are the least liquid form of asset, a high inventory turnover ratio is generally positive. On the other hand, a ratio that's unusually high compared with the average for your industry could mean you're losing sales because stock on hand is inadequate.

Just Do It

Smart Managing

It doesn't matter how you start using financial ratios. Just start using them. Depending on your primary managerial responsibilities, some ratios may be more relevant than others. Start with those.

If you're in operations, the turnover ratios will be of immediate interest. If you're in sales, knowing about liquidity and profitability ratios will help you assess a client. How many times have you chased after a business, only to find out they couldn't or wouldn't pay? If you're in purchasing, it helps to know how stable your vendors are. Have any ever failed to deliver?

Inventory to Net Working Capital

This ratio tells how much of the company's funds are tied up in inventory.

$$\text{inventory to net working capital} = \frac{\text{inventory}}{\text{net working capital}}$$

If this number is high compared with the industry average, it could mean the business has too much inventory on hand. It's preferable to run your business with as little inventory as possible on hand, as long as it doesn't mean losing out on potential sales opportunities.

Debt Ratios

Debt ratios measure the extent to which a firm relies on debt to finance its operations. Various types of debt from the liabilities section of the balance sheet are compared with various assets. These ratios are useful for comparing changes—growth or decline—in a company's performance from one period to another and within an industry. They're also commonly called *leverage ratios,* in reference to the power that can come from the appropriate use of debt financing.

Debt-to-Assets Ratio

This ratio, sometimes known simply as *debt ratio,* shows the extent to which a company is financed with debt.

$$\text{debt-to-assets ratio} = \frac{\text{total liabilities}}{\text{total assets}}$$

The higher this ratio, the more the business is financed by outside creditors. The firm is more highly leveraged (debt) and a higher risk for creditors. Generally, this calculation ignores short-term obligations (e.g. current liabilities) in calculating debt ratios based on the prior four quarters of financial performance.

Debt-to-Equity Ratio

This ratio measures the percentage of debt tied up in the owner's equity. Generally, this calculation uses only long-term debt.

$$\text{debt-to-equity ratio} = \frac{\text{long-term debt}}{\text{total equity}}$$

As a rule of thumb, a high debt-to-equity ratio means a firm is more capital-intensive, with all the risks that entails. If this number is high, the company may want to look for ways to cut the debt load. Highly leveraged companies are usually more vulnerable to business downturns than those with lower debt-to-equity ratios.

Times Interest Earned

Times interest earned, sometimes called the *interest coverage ratio,* measures the creditworthiness of a company, the ability of the company to meet its debt payments. The ratio shows how many times a company could pay the interest on the annual debt load. The higher the times interest earned, the more likely the firm can meet its obligations.

$$\text{times interest earned} = \frac{\text{earnings before interest and taxes (EBIT)}}{\text{interest}}$$

The EBIT is the operating profit from the income statement. For the denominator, use the interest expense from the prior four quarters.

Fixed Payment Coverage Ratio

The fixed payment coverage ratio includes the principal plus interest amount owed to creditors. It's another measure of the ability to repay debt.

$$\text{fixed payment coverage ratio} = \frac{\text{EBIT}}{\text{interest} + (\text{principal} + \text{preferred dividends}) \times [1-(1 \, / \, \text{tax rate})]}$$

The higher the ratio, the safer creditors are in receiving amounts owed to them.

Profitability Ratios

The profitability ratios track how well the firm generates a profit through its operations. Since profitability is the core measurement of a going concern, several ratios have been developed to dissect profits.

Gross Profit Margin (GPM)

The gross profit margin subtracts the costs of goods sold as a measure of sales to give the first indication of how much profit is left to cover overhead and other cash items. Calculate GPM using the prior four quarters.

$$\text{gross profit margin} = \frac{(\text{sales} - \text{cost of goods sold})}{\text{sales}}$$

A high GPM suggests that the firm has good cost management controls of its operations. A high GPM indicates that a business can make a reasonable profit on sales, as long as it keeps overhead costs in control. If business is slow and profits are weak, a high margin could indicate overpricing. A low GPM, especially relative to industry norms, could indicate underpricing. In general, the GPM should be stable, not fluctuating much from period to period, unless the industry has been undergoing changes that affect the costs of goods sold or pricing policies.

Operating Profit Margin (OPM)

The operating profit margin indicates how effective a company is at controlling the costs and expenses of its operations. The remaining deductions are interest and taxes.

$$\text{operating profit margin} = \frac{\text{EBIT}}{\text{sales}}$$

Like GPM, the higher the OPM, the more pricing flexibility a company has in its operations. This pricing flexibility provides greater safety during tough economic times. A higher OPM could also be a sign of the degree of cost control management.

Net Profit Margin (NPM)

Net profit margin is one of the key performance indicators. The higher the net profit margin, the more effectively the company is converting revenue into profit. The NPM measures the profits available to shareholders after deducting interest and taxes.

$$\text{net profit margin} = \frac{\text{net profits}}{\text{sales}}$$

Comparing profit with sales volume is useful. You can determine whether you're making enough of a profit. The higher the profit margin, the more pricing flexibility a firm may have in its operations or the greater cost control initiated by management.

Return on Investment (ROI)

Return on investment shows how well a company uses its assets to generate profits.

return on investment = total assets turnover x net profit margin

The DuPont formula is often used to determine the return on investment. The DuPont method allows the firm to break down its return on investment into two parts—a profit on sales and an indicator of efficient asset use. Typically, a low net profit margin (NPM) means a high total asset turnover (TAT). The significance of the relationship between the NPM and TAT, however, is largely dependent on the industry.

Return on Assets (ROA)

This ratio tells how effectively a business has been making its assets work. The ROA measures the use of capital to make profit (before interest and income tax).

$$\text{return on assets} = \frac{\text{EBIT}}{\text{net operating assets}}$$

This ratio is most useful when compared with the interest rate paid on the company's debt. When the cost of borrowing— the interest rate—is higher than the benefit of doing business— the ROA, there's a problem. For example, if the ROA is 10% and the interest rate paid on its debt is 12%, the business's profit was 2% lower than the interest it paid to make that profit: it's costing money to stay in business.

Return on Equity (ROE)

This ratio measures the return earned by a company on its equity. It has the most narrowly defined capital base of the profitability ratios. The higher the rate, the more the company has increased the wealth of its shareholders.

$$\text{return on equity} = \frac{\text{net profits}}{\text{shareholder equity}}$$

It should be noted that financial analysts vary somewhat in calculating return on equity.

Earnings per Share (EPS)

The earnings per share measures the dollar return per share to owners of a company.

$$\text{earnings per share} = \frac{\text{total earnings}}{\text{shares outstanding}}$$

As with many of these ratios, EPS can be calculated broadly through the use of plain balance sheet numbers or by subtracting out earnings components or calculating the weighted average of shares outstanding. This depends on the analytical relationships you seek to establish.

Putting It All Together

There are a number of other valuable ratios that haven't been covered here. Among these we could mention *price/earnings ratio, price-to-sales ratio,* and *price-to-book-value ratio,* primarily because they're more relevant to investing activities than to managing a business. As you develop your understanding, you may find other ratios to depend on to boost your managerial career.

Now for a little test. The income statement and balance sheet for General Widget, Inc. are shown below. Following these reports is a matrix of ratio analysis and the formulas. Take the numbers from the statements and calculate the ratios. What kind of shape is General Widget in?

Income Statement
General Widget, Inc.
December 31, 200_

(Account Names)	(Account Sums)	(Aggregated Sums and Totals)
Sales Revenues		3,500,000
Cost of Sales		
Materials	575,000	
Labor	625,000	
Overhead	250,000	1,450,000
Gross Margin		2,050,000
Operating Expense		
Selling	450,000	
General and Administrative	350,000	
Depreciation and Amortization	100,000	900,000
Operating Income		1,150,000
Other Income and Expenses		
Dividends and Interest	25,000	
Interest Expense	(75,000)	
Unusual/Extraordinary Items	150,000	100,000
Income Before Tax		1,050,000
Income Tax (t = .34)		357,000
Net Revenues		693,000

Balance Sheet
General Widget, Inc.
December 31, 200_

Assets	
Current Assets	
Cash	350,000
Accounts Receivable	500,000
Marketable Securities	68,000
Inventory	444,400
Prepaid Expenses	15,000
Total Current Assets	1,377,400

General Widget, Inc.
Balance Sheet
December 31, 200_

Assets	
Property, Plant, Equipment	
Land	600,000
Buildings	1,100,000
Machinery	1,390,000
Furniture and Fixtures	300,000
Vehicles	315,000
Accumulated Depreciation	95,000
Net Property, Plant, Equipment	3,800,000
Total Assets	5,177,400
Liabilities	
Current Liabilities	
Accounts Payable	580,000
Notes Payable	199,000
Accrued Expenses	95,000
Income Taxes Payable	43,400
Total Current Liabilities	917,400
Long-Term Liabilities	
Deferred Taxes	350,000
Long-Term Debt	2,000,000
Total Liabilities	3,267,400
Shareholder Equity	
Preferred Stock	200,000
Common Stock	1,190,000
Paid-in Capital	420,000
Retained Earnings	100,000
Total Shareholder Equity	1,910,000
Total Liabilities and Shareholder Equity	5,177,400

Test your knowledge of financial ratios. Using this matrix, calculate the General Widget numbers on page 81. Round to two decimal places. In calculating average payment period, use direct materials for purchases. Use 10% as the interest rate or cost of capital. (The answers are in the Resources section at the end of the book.)

Ratio	Formula	Answer
Current	$$\frac{\text{Current Assets}}{\text{Current Liabilities}}$$	
Quick (Acid)	$$\frac{\text{Current Assets} - \text{Inventory}}{\text{Current Liabilities}}$$	
Net Working Capital	Current Assets $-$ Current Liabilities	
Accounts Collection Period	$$\frac{\text{Accounts Receivable}}{\text{Sales} / 360 \text{ days}}$$	
Average Payment Period	$$\frac{\text{Accounts Payable}}{\text{Purchases} / 360 \text{ days}}$$	
Fixed Assets Turnover	$$\frac{\text{Sales}}{\text{Fixed Assets}}$$	
Total Assets Turnover	$$\frac{\text{Sales}}{\text{Total Assets}}$$	
Inventory Turnover	$$\frac{\text{Cost of Goods Sold}}{\text{Total Inventory}}$$	
Inventory to Net Working Capital	$$\frac{\text{Inventory}}{\text{Net Working Capital}}$$	
Debt-to-Assets	$$\frac{\text{Total Liabilities}}{\text{Total Assets}}$$	
Debt-to-Equity	$$\frac{\text{Long-Term Debt}}{\text{Total Equity}}$$	
Times Interest Earned	$$\frac{\text{EBIT}}{\text{Interest}}$$	
Gross Profit Margin	$$\frac{\text{Sales - Cost of Goods Sold}}{\text{Sales}}$$	
Operating Profit Margin	$$\frac{\text{EBIT}}{\text{Sales}}$$	
Net Profit Margin	$$\frac{\text{Net Profit}}{\text{Sales}}$$	
Return on Investment	Total Assets Turnover x Net Profit Margin	
Return on Equity	$$\frac{\text{Net Profit}}{\text{Shareholder Equity}}$$	

Manager's Checklist for Chapter 4

❏ Financial ratios are one of the best and simplest ways to set an objective performance standard.

❏ To be meaningful, financial ratios must be viewed in comparison with the ratios of other entities with similar characteristics.

❏ Liquidity ratios measure short-term solvency. Higher numbers show strength.

❏ Operational ratios show how efficiently a company uses its assets. Generally, higher numbers show strength.

❏ Leverage ratios show how much the company uses debt financing. Generally, lower numbers show strength.

❏ Profitability ratios measure how well the firm generates profits. Generally, higher numbers show strength.

Management Accounting

A nd now, for something completely different ... management accounting!

Up to now, our focus has been on what is termed *financial* accounting. Financial accounting information concentrates on meeting the needs of external parties such as bankers and investors. These accounting disclosures of business operations help determine investment and lending decisions. A variety of federal and local government laws require you to collect, process, and report the financial information. The outside analysts receive management's financial information in prescribed formats that are generally equivalent from company to company. Straying from these laws exposes management to sanctions, fines, and imprisonment.

Financial accounting deals with past events. The information often summarizes results at a high level. Using the notion that the past is prologue, its analytical tools project the future based on the results of past actions. Financial accounting ratio analysis helps show performance trends and predict the future

Smart Managing

Financial Accounting

As mentioned in Chapter 1, financial accounting is the face your business shows the outside world, through the financial statements that are prepared for banks, stockholders, investors, and government agencies. These financial statements are basically historical records that cover a particular time period, including balance sheet, income statement, statement of cash flow, and statement of shareholders' equity.

assuming a steady state, that tomorrow will be much like yesterday. The limitations of such analysis quickly become apparent when you consider the host of dynamic management questions you face every day—lease or buy? when to increase inventory? what is the best selling price? how many do I have to sell? can this job be bid profitably? and so forth.

Management Accounting—for the Future

Since the Ancients first gazed into bird guts to guide their actions, leaders have sought ways to catch the future at its flood and ride it to profit and glory. In today's business world, the practice of management accounting is the path to future insight. Notice I said, "practice." Experience is an effective instructor, even if sometimes cruel. Management accounting is, above all else, the search for relationships and patterns, patterns that will lead to a competitive advantage. Those patterns can be hard to find. Once found, they can also vanish into thin air. It is a daily challenge.

For a formal definition, management accounting involves identifying, collecting, sorting, estimating, and analyzing cost, performance, and other information to make timely decisions. The time reference is on decisions to plan and control the future. Budgets, forecasts, and estimates, while based on historic data retrieved from the accounting system, guide future management actions. The perspective, unlike financial reporting, gives detailed analysis to smaller parts of the entity and intertwining relationships. It can divide and/or compare the data by products, regions, delivery channel, etc.

How all this information is put to meaningful use is as much art as science. While there are certainly AICPA and individual industry recommendations on the methodology of management accounting, there are many ways

> **Management accounting** *Key Term*
> The practice of identifying, collecting, sorting, estimating, and analyzing cost, performance, and other information to make timely decisions and to plan and control the future through budgets, forecasts, and estimates.

to meet the individual needs of the business managers. Unlike the hard, clear edges of financial accounting, no one way can be named the best, although consultants will evangelize for a fee. The choice is among approaches that have proved more or less useful for your business size and industry.

One thing shines clear. You must do something. To survive in today's global environment, you have to pay attention to key elements of management

> **Cost behavior** The man- *Key Term*
> ner in which a cost changes as the related activity changes. Some costs vary with volume or operational expenses; others remain constant.

accounting. It is your understanding of *cost behavior* that will set you right on the path to business success. Without such an understanding, you might as well be casting runes.

Cost Accounting

Management accounting is often called *cost* accounting and you will find the terms used interchangeably. Cost accounting is generally considered the major subset of management accounting. The field of cost accounting has most of the analytical theories and approaches to cost behavior. To make a distinction, management accounting looks to the tasks of decision-making, policy setting, and communicating information, while cost accounting collects and analyzes costing, pricing, and performance details for internal management and, crossing into financial accounting, for external reporting.

Management accounting systems can report information in any way that is useful to management. The system does not have to conform to GAAP.

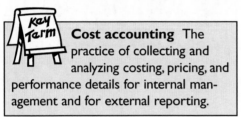

Cost accounting The practice of collecting and analyzing costing, pricing, and performance details for internal management and for external reporting.

Unfortunately, once the data is in the system, it is often unused or misused. Managers are usually aware of what is in the externally reported financials. What happens then is that managers use only the information in external financial reports—and so they make poor decisions. Successful managers need to learn, through study or experience, the tools to find and analyze the relevant data necessary to make good business decisions.

Cost accounting developed from three data streams.

The first might be termed desperate experience. This branch is perhaps best exemplified by breakeven calculations, discussed more fully in this chapter, and production/overhead/inventory management, discussed in the next.

The second stems from academic research. Here you will find such concepts as activity-based costing (ABC), balanced scorecard, and transfer pricing, all discussed in a later chapter.

Finally, there is the constructed software package approach, ranging from Intuit's QuickBooks® and Microsoft's Small Business Manager, through Solomon and MAS90®, to the enterprise behemoths like SAAP R3/R4, PeopleSoft, and Baan.

⚠ CAUTION!

Choice or Confusion?

In this multiplicity of approaches lie both opportunity and danger. Choosing an inappropriate cost or management accounting system can quickly lead to financial or competitive ruin. Pick a middle-of-the-pack approach and you will get middling results. Chose the optimum one for your situation and you may enjoy a significant competitive advantage over other companies. You will find yourself making smarter investment, inventory, pricing, and hiring decisions and making them faster.

Management Accounting and Competition

Sometimes a management accounting system can create a huge competitive advantage. Consider SABRE (Semi-Automated Business Research Environment), the reservation system developed by American Airlines. This was a management accounting system that let AA manage its yield and pricing to crushing competitive advantage. SABRE was so effective that competitors had to mount a series of lawsuits to slow AA while they built their own systems. AA was still able to grow and then maintain its status as one of the two dominant U.S. domestic airlines. As the SABRE innovations became more widespread throughout the industry, AA was able to spin off SABRE at a handsome profit while relying on new initiatives to maintain its competitive position.

Aside from some general observations about management accounting systems, the package approaches are not covered in this book. While each system can capture and sift, with varying degrees of felicity, the raw data necessary for cost analysis, it is not until you get into enterprise-level software that you go much beyond standard financial reporting capability. You still have to extract the relevant data and process it separately. The determined manager will find a way to extract and use the data.

Cost accounting varies, depending on whether you manufacture or retail goods and on whether you provide a product or a service. In each area, the approach to cost identification varies. The goal of all approaches is to aid strategic decision-making and cost management. There are some constants that you need to understand in order to talk about cost accounting. You will want to know how much you have to sell to meet expenses. You will want to know the effect of pricing on sales volume.

In just about all systems, you want to find what it cost to operate and maintain the business and the amount of profit made within a specific time period. If you manufacture, you will want to know the value of the raw materials and the work in process. How much did you make from finished goods sold and how many remain to be sold? You take those results and prepare for the activities of the next time period. You make budgets and forecasts. You compare with past time periods and look at any variances that might need corrective action or improvement. These results help you control, plan, and decide.

The Vocabulary of Cost Accounting

Many of the cost accounting terms are fuzzy and imprecise. You can find them defined differently in several sources. For our purposes, we will use the following definitions.

Cost The cash, cash equivalents, or resources spent to reach a specific objective.

Cost center A location or function of an organization where management is primarily responsible for controlling costs.

Cost drivers Output measures of resources and activities. Hours worked drive labor wage costs. How well the top managers identify the most appropriate cost drivers determines how well they understand cost behavior and how well costs are controlled.

Cost object Any activity, item, or operation for which management wants a separate cost measurement. Examples of cost objects are a product, a service, a project, a customer, a brand category, a department, or a program.

Cost unit A quantitative unit of product or service for which costs are known. (See *cost object.*)

Direct costs Costs tied specifically or traced to a given cost object. Examples are direct materials (DM), direct labor (DL), and direct expenses (DE).

Fixed costs Costs not immediately affected by changes in the cost driver, staying the same regardless of volume. Most balance sheet fixed assets represent fixed costs.

Indirect costs Costs that cannot be tied specifically or traced to a given cost object. Examples are indirect materials (IDM), indirect labor (IDL), and indirect expenses (IDE).

Mixed costs Costs with both fixed and variable components. An example might be marketing costs that have a budgeted base but then rise and fall as sales change.

Profit center A location or function of an organization where management is primarily responsible for generating profits.

Relevant range The range of costs through which the cost/volume/profit relationship holds generally true. Usually, it is within two standard deviations or less.

Variable costs Costs that change in direct proportion to changes in the cost driver. For example, wages payable vary as hours worked wax and wane.

Cost/Volume/Profit Analysis

If you bought this book for no other reason than this next section, you will be well rewarded. Go into several businesses with gross sales less than $10 million. Ask the managers or owners what their breakeven point is. You will be lucky if you find 20% who know it. If that is the case, you probably went into several franchised businesses. Most franchisors stress breakeven analysis. Your number will probably be around 5% or 10%.

Do you know your own business's breakeven? If you do, congratulations! You'll probably also notice that the other managers and owners who know their breakeven have thriving businesses too. If you do not know your breakeven, not to worry: you are about to become a forecasting commando.

I would pick the concept of breakeven as the single most important business concept to grasp. Even with its limitations, and we'll cover those, once you understand that tiny point that teeters on the margin of profit and loss, you are on your way to becoming a master.

Breakeven point The volume of sales needed for a business to cover all of its expenses (fixed and variable), to generate zero profit. As an equation, breakeven point = fixed costs ÷ gross margin percentage.

Now, most business owners, through experience, do get a notion of where their breakeven is. "I have to gross around $250,000 a year before I can start to feel comfortable," you might hear them say. Ask them how much they would need to open another store, start another crew, or add a new line of business and the answer will be less precise. For a strong and successful business, you must know the financial impact of your most basic business decisions.

What happens if your sales volume drops? How low can it go before you see red ink? If you chop your prices to sell more, how much more will you have to sell? What are your most profitable products or services? If you or the sales force push them, how much more will you make? Enough to expand? If you take out a loan to expand and the interest forces fixed costs up, what sales volume will cover those increased costs?

The breakeven equation (BE) and related cost/volume/profit (CVP) analysis corollaries can answer these questions and many more about your business operations. BE/CVP analysis looks at the relationship among your fixed and variable costs, your volume (in terms of units or in terms of dollars), and your profits.

> **Key Term**
>
> **Cost/volume/profit (CVP) analysis** A way of examining the relationship among your costs (fixed and variable), your volume (as units or as dollars), and your profits.

The two principal breakeven (BE) analysis formulas are:

breakeven sales volume = fixed costs ÷ contribution margin ratio

breakeven sales dollars = gross sales − variable costs − fixed costs

The contribution margin ratio is sales price (SP) minus variable costs (VC). The contribution margin (CM) is gross sales (S) minus VC. This remainder contains the fixed costs (FC) plus any profit.

> **Tricks of the Trade**
>
> ## CVP Basics
>
> There are three main tools offered by CVP analysis:
> - *Breakeven analysis* tells you the sales volume in units or dollars you need to break even, in various price or cost scenarios.
> - *Contribution margin analysis* compares the profitability of different products, lines, or services.
> - *Operating leverage* is a measure of how your business uses fixed costs. High operating leverage magnifies profits as sales rise and losses as sales drop.

Profit (P) alone could be stated as
$$P = CM - FC$$
Thus, when profit is zero, the breakeven point, $S - VC - FC$, = 0. Expressed algebraically, the BE sales volume equation is
$$BE \text{ (units)} = FC \div (SP - VC)$$
Let's take an example to put our equations to work. Assume the following facts:

- fixed costs (FC) = $40,000
- selling price per unit (SP) = $10
- variable cost per unit (VC) = $6

Let's stick those values into our equation, BE (units) = FC ÷ (SP – VC).

- BE (units) = 40,000 ÷ (10 – 6)
- BE (units) = 40,000 ÷ 4
- BE (units) = 10,000 units

If the selling price is $10 per unit, the breakeven in sales dollars is 10,000 units multiplied by $10 per unit. We need $100,000 in gross sales revenue to reach breakeven.

An algebraic alternative to solving for the breakeven point in sales dollars is to let X equal breakeven sales in dollars, so that the equation

sales (BE$) = gross sales – fixed costs – variable costs

is expressed in our example as:

$0 = X - 0.6X - \$40,000$

$X - 0.6X = \$40,000$ (solving for X)

$0.4X = \$40,000$

$X = \$100,000$

You can check this result with a variable cost income statement.

Gross Sales (10,000 × $10) $100,000

Less: Variable costs (10,000 × $6) 60,000

Fixed costs 40,000

CVP Assumptions

Smart
Managing
• The behavior of gross sales revenue is linear over the relevant range.
• The behavior of total costs is linear over the relevant range.
• Costs can be categorized as fixed, variable, or mixed.
• Capacity stays constant during the reference period.
• Labor and technology productivity and market conditions do not change.
• For both variable and fixed costs, sales volume is the only cost driver.
• The sales mix remains constant over the relevant range.
• For manufacturing firms, inventory stays the same from beginning to end of the relevant period.

Profit before taxes 0

Less: Income taxes 0

Profit after taxes $0

Now that you understand how to calculate breakeven, you can plan for profit. What sales in units and dollars are needed to reach a target profit before taxes of $50,000?

Let X = breakeven point in units.

Sales = $10X

Less: Variable costs = 6X

Contribution margin $90,000 = $4X (Remember: CM = P + FC.)

Less: Fixed costs $40,000

Profit before taxes $50,000

Therefore, $90,000 = $4X

22,500 units = X

Sales in dollars = 22,500 × $10 = $225,000.

Check this by completing the variable cost income statement.

Sales $225,000 = 22,500 × $10

Less: Variable costs − 135,000 = 22,500 × $6

Contribution margin $90,000

Less: Fixed costs 40,000

Profit before taxes $50,000

> ### How Changes in Fixed Costs, Variable Costs, and Price Behave
> Smart Managing
> - Breakeven changes in the same direction as a change in fixed costs: as fixed costs go up, breakeven goes up.
> - Breakeven changes in the same direction as a change in variable costs: as variable costs go up, breakeven goes up.
> - Breakeven changes in the opposite direction as a change in selling price: as selling price goes up, breakeven goes down.

Let's toss taxes into the mix. We'll assume a tax rate of 35%. What unit and dollar sales do you need to reach a targeted after-tax profit of $30,000? Let's set up what we know.

Let X = breakeven point in units.

Sales $ = $10X

Less: Variable costs = 6X

Contribution margin = $4X

Less: Fixed costs 40,000

Profit before taxes $

Less income taxes $

Profit after taxes $30,000

To calculate profit *after* taxes (AFTER), start by finding the profit *before* taxes (BEFORE).

AFTER = (1 − tax rate) × BEFORE

$30,000 = (1 − .35) × BEFORE

$30,000 ÷ .65 = BEFORE

$46,154 = BEFORE

Therefore, Sales $ = $10X

Less: Variable costs = $6X

Contribution margin $86,154 = $4X

Less: Fixed costs 40,000

Profit before taxes $46,154

Less: Income taxes 16,154 = 35% × $46,154

Profit after taxes $30,000

$4X = $86,154

X = \$86,154 ÷ \$4

X = 21,538.5 units (You won't sell half a unit, so round up.)

Sales in dollars = 21,539 x \$10 or \$215,390

The income statement below shows that \$215,390 in sales will get you an after-tax profit of \$30,000 after rounding.

Sales \$215,390

Less: Variable costs 129,234

Contribution margin \$86,156

Less: Fixed costs 40,000

Profit before taxes \$46,156

Less: Income taxes 16,155

Profit after taxes \$30,001

Limitations of BE/CVP Analysis

Given the assumptions surrounding BE/CVP analysis listed earlier, you should understand that many of them create real-world limitations associated with BE/CVP analysis.

The analysis assumes a linear sales function and a linear cost function. Costs in particular can move in stair-step fashion with increased volume. The level of output can affect both selling price and variable costs. This creates nonlinear relationships, resulting in two or more breakeven points.

The analysis assumes that price, total fixed costs, and unit variable costs can be clearly identified and stay steady over the relevant range. This area is one of the hardest to pin down, as quantities and values are constantly shifting. If mixed costs cannot be separated into fixed and variable, breakeven results will be inaccurate and of limited use.

The analysis assumes that you sell all inventory or production. Unsold inventory makes breakeven calculations moot. Also, the BE/CVP analysis does not recognize cash flow. It assumes only short-term profit planning. It considers neither the time value of money nor the timing of revenues and costs.

For multiple-product analysis, you know the product sales mix. Rarely will customers buy in exactly the product mix ratios you calculate. You can determine the contribution margin only for a particular product mix. If the product mix actually sold differs from that used in the analysis, expected profit and realized profit will be different.

Management could perform BE/CVP analysis separately for each product. It could be hard to allocate common fixed costs of all product lines to each single product line.

You assume to know the selling prices and costs over the relevant range. There are a number of factors, particularly involved in overhead calculations, as we shall learn in the next chapter, that make these figures less certain.

In many situations, more sophisticated mathematical tools, to include calculus and linear programming, can be used to reach similar results. The BE/CVP analyses work best for firms, branches, or product lines with sales less than $8-$10 million. Beyond that range, you will need more sophisticated forecasting tools.

Do you want to set a profit target for your sales force? What gross sales figure in dollars will they have to reach for a pretax profit equal to 25% of sales?

Let X = sales in dollars

Sales $ = 1.0X

Less: Variable costs = 0.6X

Contribution margin $40,000 + .25X = 0.4X

Less: Fixed costs $40,000

Profit before taxes .25X

.4X = $40,000 + .25X

.15X = $40,000

X = $40,000 ÷ .15

X = $267,000 (after rounding up)

Use the variable cost income statement to test the solution.

Sales $ 267,000

Less: Variable costs 160,200 = .6 ($267,000)

Contribution margin $106,800 = .4 ($267,000)

Less: Fixed costs 40,000

Profit before taxes $66,800

With rounding, $66,800 is 25% of $267,000. Come on, folks! That's a doable target.

OK, we're getting hot now. What sales in dollars do we need

to hit a targeted after-tax profit of 8% of sales? This is the kind of number the Board of Directors or CEO sets up. You wonder where they got it. I can assure you it was set only after the most careful deliberation, considering all relevant economic, social, and market factors. Trust me.

Let X = sales in dollars

Sales $ = 1.0X

Less: Variable costs = 0.6X

Contribution margin $ = 0.4X

Less: Fixed costs 40,000

Profit before taxes $

Less: Income taxes

Profit after taxes $.08X

We've done something like this before, so it should be getting easier. Remember: this takes practice.

AFTER = (1 − tax rate) x BEFORE

0.08X = (1 − .35) x BEFORE

0.08X ÷ 0.65 = BEFORE

0.123X = BEFORE

Therefore,

Sales $ = 1.0X

Less: Variable costs = 0.6X

Contribution margin $ 40,000 +.123X = 0.4X

Less: Fixed costs 40,000

Profit before taxes 0.123X

Less: Income taxes 0.35 X

Profit after taxes 0.08 X

.4X = 40,000 + .123X

.277X = 40,000

X = $40,000 ÷ .277

X = $144,404

The following income statement checks the solution:

Sales $144,404

Less: Variable costs 86,643 = .6 x $144,404

Contribution margin $57,761

Less: Fixed costs 40,000

Profit before taxes $17,761

Less: Income taxes 6,216 = .35 x $17,761

Profit after taxes $11,545= .08 x $144,404 (after rounding)

Hey, that wasn't so hard. As a bonus, your sales target is now actually lower than the 25% of pretax sales you set earlier. Now for some graduate school work. Here's an example using multiple products with different contribution margins.

Product SP – VC = CM x Mix = CM

A $10 – $6 = $4 x 3 = $12

B $8 – $5 = $3 x 2 = $6

Total CM per package $18

Given: Total A and B fixed costs = $180,000

BE (units) X = Fixed cost / Unit contribution margin

   = $180,000 / $18

   = 10,000 packages to break even

Since each package contains three units of A and two units of B, to break even, we need to sell:

A: 3 x 10,000 = 30,000 units

B: 2 x 10,000 = 20,000 units

Operating Leverage

Operating leverage measures how much a firm or project relies on fixed rather than variable costs. Picture a teeter-totter: one end is sales and the other is profit. Here's what operating leverage looks like:

Contribution Margin Is Key

TRICKS OF THE TRADE

If you face any limitations on the quantity of products that can be produced or sold, then you gain the greatest total profit through concentrating on those products that yield the highest contribution margin in relation to the limiting factor.

$$\frac{\text{Revenue} \qquad\qquad\qquad\qquad \text{Profit}}{\text{(OL)}}$$

As you can see, the fulcrum is shifted well off-center toward the revenue side. That means that if you push down on the revenue side of the lever the profit side will obviously move up much more than the corresponding push down. That's operating leverage—a unit increase in revenue results in a multi-unit increase in profit.

Increased leverage means replacing variable costs with fixed costs. Operating leverage implies replacing labor with capital, workers with machines. Greater operating leverage increases profits when sales are high, since variable costs are lower and the contribution margin is increased. Conversely, when most of the costs are fixed, then the costs will remain high while sales are dropping and profits shrink. This is why profits often shoot up after a retrenchment. Companies have cut variable costs to survive, so when sales increase again, profits outpace the addition of variable costs.

There is some controversy within the accounting profession about how operating leverage should be determined. For our purposes, we'll use the following formula:

degree of operating leverage =
contribution margin ÷ profit before taxes (aka operating income)

(DOL = CM / OI)

⚠ CAUTION!

Operating Leverage Cuts Both Ways

The risk in high fixed costs is that the business must keep sales high. A small error in forecasting sales can be magnified into large errors in cash flow and threaten the existence of the firm if fixed costs can't be covered.

Smaller service and retail businesses tend to have fewer employees and so often treat payroll as a fixed cost. The owners and managers would like to avoid the turmoil, administrative, and training costs that layoffs bring. This means smaller businesses must operate efficiently with these relatively higher fixed costs. Insufficient cash flow (often caused by high fixed costs) and high fixed costs are the leading causes of small business failures.

The result is a ratio. From our example above where we calculated the sales in dollars needed to hit a targeted after-tax
profit of 8% of sales:

degree of operating leverage = $57,761 ÷ $17,761 = 3.25

Now suppose that sales are 25% higher than projected.
What is the percentage change in profits?

Percentage change in profits = DOL x percentage change in sales

Percentage change in profits = 3.25 x 25% = 81%

Proof: Sales $144,404

Less: Variable costs 86,643 = .6 x $144,404

Contribution margin $57,761

Less: Fixed costs 40,000

Profit before taxes $17,761

Sales $180,505

Less: Variable costs 108,303 = .6 x $180,505

Contribution margin $72,202

Less: Fixed costs 40,000

Profit before taxes $32,202

Degree of operating leverage = $72,202 ‚ $32,202 = 2.24

Profit before taxes increases by 81%, $17,761 x 1.81 =
$32,202 (with rounding). The DOL drops to 2.24 because the
variable costs also increased.

Assume now that the company buys two machines that
increase fixed costs to $30,000. These same machines can cut
variable costs by $.20 per unit, bringing variable costs down to
$.40 per unit.

Sales $180,505

Less: Variable costs 72,202 = .4 x $180,505

Contribution margin $108,303

Less: Fixed costs 70,000

Profit before taxes $38,303

Degree of operating leverage = $108,303 ÷ $38,303 = 2.83

Profit before taxes increases almost 20 % over the high-
variable-cost scenario ($38,303 versus $32,202). The DOL

goes up to 2.83 because the variable costs are now lowered. This example also gives you an idea of the power of changes in the contribution margin that can come from controlling both variable and fixed costs.

Margin of Safety

The margin of safety tells you how low sales can fall before creating a loss. The margin of safety equals sales minus breakeven sales (MOS = S − BE$). Select a desired margin of safety in terms of sales, either by forecast or actual numbers. Calculate the breakeven point in dollars. The difference indicates how far sales can fall before reaching the breakeven point. The range is your margin of safety.

Assume that a company has the following projected income statement:

Sales $100,000

Less: Variable expenses 60,000

Contribution margin 40,000

Less: Fixed expenses 30,000

Income before taxes $10,000

The breakeven point in dollars (BE$) is equal to $30,000 ÷ .4 or $75,000. The safety margin equals $100,000 - $75,000 or $25,000.

Benefits of BE/CVP

As you become more sensitive to the movements in fixed and variable costs on contribution margin and profit, you will find several benefits in using BE/CVP on a regular basis. You will have firmer grasp on analyzing the impact that volume has on short-term profits. Also the changes in costs, both variable and fixed, have an impact on profit. You will also understand how changing the selling price through changing the contribution margin will affect the amount you have to sell and your operating income. When you are working with multiple products, it can help you analyze how the mix affects profits.

CVP analysis is merely a simplified model. The usefulness of CVP analysis may be greater in less complex smaller firms. For larger firms, CVP analysis can be valuable as a decision tool for the planning stages of new projects and ventures.

Manager's Checklist for Chapter 5

❏ Management accounting is as much art as science. You will have to practice and closely follow the behavior of patterns in the daily flow of business operations.

❏ Cost accounting is free form, compared with financial accounting. Many managers never make the transition to understanding it and so fall into the trap of looking only at revenues, expenses, and financial statements.

❏ Breakeven and cost/volume/profit analysis are your Swiss Army knife of basic analytical tools. Understanding how they work is the foundation of your operational management decision process.

❏ There are limitations to traditional BE/CVP analysis. It is as important to understand them as it is to understand the benefits.

❏ Operating leverage can be an effective tool in managing profits.

Management Cost Accounting

B reakeven and its related cost/volume/profit concepts apply to all profit-making activities. In this chapter we'll discuss inventory and overhead, two important topics.

Cost Behavior, Inventory, and Overhead

Understanding inventory costing is another part of cost accounting that affects primarily business managers. Inventory in merchandising, where you buy a finished good to sell to customers, is more straightforward than inventory in manufacturing, where you have three levels of inventory to track, as we'll discuss shortly.

Managers at all levels of government, educational institutions, and nonprofit organizations join businesses in tackling the fundamental concept of overhead. In a standard accounting textbook, overhead is usually defined as the sum of all costs after direct materials and labor have been subtracted. But that's just the tip of the iceberg.

How inventory and overhead are tracked and recorded has an impact on both the income statement and the balance sheet. When factors like net income or return on investment serve as compensation criteria, managers will strive to push those numbers into the bonus range. For example, many managers get performance bonuses if they meet certain net income targets. Since inventory is valued on the balance sheet as an asset and is not reported as an expense on the income statement until it is sold, keeping inventory at a high level can increase net income. Bonus time!

Your cost accounting approach to inventory and overhead will vary depending on whether you make or provide a product or a service. Added considerations include the performance metrics standards managers must meet. Generally, multiple performance standards reflect performance better than a single

> **Key Term**
>
> **Overhead** The costs of doing business other than direct materials and direct labor. Overhead includes rent, insurance, heat, light, supervision costs, facilities maintenance, and indirect materials and indirect labor.

> **CAUTION!**
>
> ### Multiple Meanings Confuse
>
> "Burden" is the term sometimes used interchangeably with "overhead" and sometimes in place of it. More often, you will find it referring to a specific set of costs that may include both fixed and variable costs—"What is your labor burden, your inventory burden, etc.?"
>
> As with many accounting terms, these multiple meanings can cause confusion unless you pin down the references. The culture of one company may refer to the payroll burden as the total payroll cost, while another may mean only the direct manufacturing labor cost. Add to this confusion the effects of globalization. Increasingly, British or other national accounting terms pop up in reports and papers with no context, particularly in manufacturing companies with global operations.
>
> You cannot take for granted that everyone at the table sees the elephant in the same way. As a manager, one of your tasks is to bring clarity to communication. Having everyone understand the same meaning is a good start.

standard. In the end, cost accounting is just a way to gauge how well managers meet their goals.

Liquid Lemons

For an overall look at how a business accounts for costs, manufacturing, labor, inventory, and overhead, let's call Dick and Jane back to their lemonade stand.

Dick and Jane make and sell a product. They are combined manufacturers and direct sellers.

They have a recipe for lemonade:

1 cup simple syrup (1 cup sugar dissolved in 1 cup water)
juice of 6 lemons
4 cups cold water
yield: five 8-ounce servings

They must buy raw materials to make the lemonade: lemons are $.10 each and sugar is $.30 a pound.

They know the bus stops on the corner every 15 minutes starting at 4 p.m., when they can open, until they have to close after the 6:15 p.m. bus to go home for supper. These hours will give them 10 selling opportunities. Five to 10 people get off each bus and start the hot walk home. They plan to sell two to five glasses of lemonade at $.50 per glass per bus. Oops, Molly and Tom want to get paid. They both want $1.00 per hour. Now, there is enough cost information to plan breakeven.

Each time the bus stops, their direct costs are $1.25. For total direct cost, in direct materials (DM), they will need six lemons and a half pound of sugar plus $.50 in direct labor (DL) times the 10 bus stops.

Direct materials
    6 lemons x $.10 x 10 = $6.00
    ½ pound sugar x $.15 x 10 = $1.50
Direct labor
    $.50 x 10 = $5.00
Total $12.50
    They will have to sell how many glasses to break even?

Without any overhead, they will have to sell 25 glasses at $.50 to break even.

Do you remember James? He was going to buy the supplies and they'll put him to work making the lemonade. Because he's a year older than Molly, he wants $1.10 per hour. He'll also work an extra hour getting the stuff from the store and setting up. So, that's 3.5 hours at $1.10, for $3.85.

We face a decision. How will we classify James' costs? Part could go to direct labor for mixing the lemonade. Part could go to administrative overhead for buying the materials. Then, maybe we ought to reconsider Molly and Tom as administrative overhead selling costs. Notice, by the way, that James' costs bring breakeven sales up to $16.35 ($12.50 + $3.85), more than halfway to the maximum sales predicted of $25.00 (5 glasses x 10 buses at $.50 per glass).

Recall the discussion about leverage and fixed costs. If they don't sell more than three glasses per bus, they're in the red. Converting Molly and Tom to variable cost items under the selling overhead could make sense. One of them may have to go home if sales aren't as brisk as planned.

If you're thinking ahead, you may have worked out that at maximum sales, Dick and Jane will gross just under $2.00 per hour. If they average only four glasses per bus, they'll make about $.90 per hour, less than their employees. At three glasses, they're in the red. This business looks like it will need some sort of capital infusion until it can establish a reliable customer base. Entrepreneurs can identify with this narrow ledge separating profit from loss.

What do they do with any lemonade left over at the end of the day? How about cleanup costs? Will people get clean glasses or use paper cups? How about those costs? How about equipment? James will need a knife to slice the lemons and a juicer. Also, something to heat the water to make the syrup and a pan for the syrup. Yeah, pitchers for the lemonade. Need a sign. Be nice to have someone do a cute graphic to catch people's attention. They can call their business "Liquid Lemons."

Need an umbrella to shade Molly and Tom so they don't get sunburned and have to file workers' compensation.

In the cycle of planning and decision-making, you can see that Dick and Jane are starting to put together elements for a master budget, a sales budget, a production budget, and an operating budget. For a more extensive look at budgeting, refer to *Budgeting for Managers* by Sid Kemp and Eric Dunbar (McGraw-Hill, 2003). I'll only touch on some specialized aspects of budgeting when discussing variances under activity-based costing and the budget impact on profit planning.

As a manager, your prime duties include asking questions about all the things that your entity needs to do the job and how much each costs. For a simple lemonade stand, Liquid Lemons shows the complications managers face when they have to consider and account for all the potential costs.

Classifying Costs

Useful cost data has several characteristics, regardless of the specific product or service involved. Costs may be classified by their nature, their relationship to production or administration unit activities, or their relationship to changes in production volume. The following box includes some basic cost categories.

Avoidable costs Costs that can be saved by not taking a given alternative.

Unavoidable costs Costs that cannot be saved.

Committed costs Costs that cannot be cut, even if the organization halts operations for a short time. They result from an organization's facility use, fixed contracts, or even its basic organization structure.

Conversion cost All direct labor costs and overhead costs to convert materials into finished products. In some cost accounting systems, it can specifically mean the costs to upgrade a cost object in value or durability.

Discretionary costs Costs that an organization chooses to incur, which management can quickly adjust up or, most often, down. Examples would be advertising and research, although the cost most often cut is training.

Engineered costs Costs that have a definitive, physical relationship to a selected measure of activity.

Financing cost Cost of interest paid on cash to support the organization.

Period costs Costs that are not product costs. All selling and administrative costs are typically considered to be period costs. Period costs are expensed on the income statement in the time period in which they are incurred.

Prime costs All direct materials and direct labor costs.

Product costs Direct materials, direct labor, and manufacturing overhead. They appear as the cost of goods sold on the income statement.

Relevant costs Costs that would no longer be incurred if a specific activity were to cease, costs that differ for alternatives being considered. They are also known as incremental or differential costs.

Irrelevant costs Costs that would not be affected by a decision between or among alternatives that would change relevant costs.

Sunk costs Costs that cannot be recovered because they occurred in the past and have no effect on decision making.

There are many ways to categorize a cost. In basic production, when we look at a cost's nature, we try to fit it in terms of the following:

- materials—direct and indirect
- labor—direct and indirect
- overhead—all the costs other than direct materials and direct labor

Trends in the manufacturing sector suggest that many costs once considered variable or overhead have become committed fixed or semivariable costs because of automation and labor union contract provisions. Service businesses also see this happening with salaries in particular.

Overhead costs can be further broken down into factory overhead, manufacturing overhead, administrative overhead, selling overhead, etc. How managers classify and treat these overhead costs can influence financial reporting. Net income is a major example we'll look at a bit later.

When costs are considered as part of the production process, we see that prime cost equals direct materials plus direct labor (PC = DM + DL). Product cost is direct (raw) material cost plus conversion cost. Recall that conversion cost is direct labor plus production overhead. Total cost is product cost plus all the administrative, selling, and distribution overhead involved plus any financing cost.

Under a cost/profit center arrangement, managers categorize costs by administrative units. They can look at factory departments like production or production services departments. Administrative departments might break out into personnel, accounting, security, and so forth or be lumped together as administrative overhead. Some other common operational subdivisions, depending on the nature of the business,

---

TRICKS OF THE TRADE

Cost Behavior Patterns

Variable costs (VC) stay constant on a per-unit basis and change in direct proportion to activity levels. Make more and the VC total goes up.

Step-variable costs are nearly variable, but go up in small steps rather than at a constant rate. Equipment maintenance is an example: as more machines work more hours, more maintenance work results. If the steps are small, you can treat the step-variable cost function as a variable cost.

Fixed costs (FC) remain constant in total, but fluctuate per unit depending on activity levels. Make more and the FC per unit will decrease.

Step-fixed costs behave as fixed costs within a wide relevant range, but change outside that range.

Semivariable (or mixed) costs have both a variable and a fixed component. They increase or decrease with activity levels, but not in direct proportion. An example would be a salesperson on a fixed salary plus commission.

Curvilinear costs cannot be represented with a straight line, but are represented with a curve showing either increasing or decreasing marginal costs. Working these out is why people take calculus.

are marketing, selling, distribution, and transportation departments. All of these will have some overhead costs associated with them.

Looking at cost behavior associated with volume, we find that product costs do not transfer from assets to expenses until the finished goods are sold. Once the goods are sold, their product costs become part of the expense item cost of goods sold (COGS). They are then matched with sales revenue and other operating overhead expenses to find operating income. Finished goods that are not sold by the end of a reporting period are treated as finished goods stock or inventory held for sale. Under the absorption cost accounting system (which I'll explain shortly), overhead costs linked to these finished goods are also assigned to the goods and not reported as expenses. Remember this point: we'll return to it later.

To predict costs, managers must understand cost behavior patterns as they plan, control, and make decisions for their organization's operation. Those costs need to be parsed out into the various cost categories for analysis. One common way to classify costs involves looking at the ledger account names and deciding whether each cost is fixed or variable or what. Rent? We pay it each month, so it must be fixed. Raw materials? The cost depends on how much we make, so it must be variable. Electricity? We have to pay something each month, but the bill depends on how much we run the machines, so it must be one of those semivariable costs.

Each cost is classified as a variable, fixed, or semivariable cost to determine how the cost will behave in the future. This classification is then adjusted based on experience. Many small businesses go no further. The weakness of this approach is that it reports only what costs have been, not what they should be.

Analyzing Cost Behavior

Cost behavior can show multivalent charms. The relationship to activity can be linear, nonlinear (zigzag), or curvilinear. There are four main techniques for splitting semivariable costs into component elements:

- high-low
- engineering
- scatter graph
- least squares regression analysis

Because all of these methods depend, to some degree, on past data, if conditions change dramatically the results will be unreliable in predicting future cost.

The *high-low* (two-point) method relies on the highest and lowest cost in a given period for prior activity levels.

The variable cost part of the mixed cost is the change in cost divided by the change in activity:

$$VC = \Delta C / \Delta A$$

(In mathematical formulas, the Greek letter delta (Δ) means change.)

The fixed cost component is equal to the total cost at high volume less the high volume times the variable cost component:

$$FC = TC - (HV \times VC)$$

In the *engineering approach*, engineers study a product's direct material and labor requirements, add related direct overhead, and then make per-unit estimates of the costs that

	Variable and Fixed Costs		
Month	**Electricity Costs**		**Units Produced**
Jan	$5,000		1,600
Feb	$2,500		1,400
Mar	$1,000		1,200

$VC = \Delta C / \Delta A$
$VC = (\$5,000 - \$1,000) / (1,600 - 1,200)$
$VC = \$4,000 / 400$
$VC = \$10.00$ per unit

$FC = \$5,000 - (1,600 \times 1.00)$
$FC = \$5,000 - 1,600$
$FC = \$3,400$

should vary with production. As a predictor, this approach shows what costs should be rather than what they were. The engineering approach is often used when making a decision on whether to start producing an item or to upgrade or otherwise alter an item. In the case of a new product, this estimate is then adjusted as operational data comes available.

A useful feature that is sometimes combined with the engineering approach and sometimes stands alone is a simple interview. Asking workers directly involved in production helps identify cost drivers and find out what's likely to happen, given specific action paths. Interviewing workers not only clarifies the engineering approach, but also has residual managerial benefits: it gives people who have firsthand experience input into the analysis.

For the *scatter graph* method, you gather cost and volume data from prior periods and chart the data points on an X-Y grid. Then, you draw a straight line from the origin to the farthest data point. The placement and slope of the line are judgment calls: you eyeball the data and fit the line visually as close to the data points as possible. Then, for any cost/volume consideration, you start from the corresponding X-Y axis, go out to the line, and then go straight over to the other axis to find the result. The scatter approach works reasonably well if you have a large number of data points.

Then, there's *regression analysis*. This is a more rigorous, statistical way to tease out the fixed and variable parts of a mixed cost. Like other methods, regression uses cost and volume data from prior periods. Regression, in many respects, is the mathematical solution to the scatter graph's guessed relationships. The equation takes the form $Y = a + bX$. For our immediate purposes, the observed dependent variable, Y, is the given semivariable cost, while a equals fixed costs, b equals variable costs, and X is the independent variable.

There are two reasons for all the fuss to clarify exactly which costs are fixed and which costs are variable. The first reason is to be able to find breakeven and, from there, do further analysis on the cost/volume/profit relationships to guide our manage-

Progress Through Regression

Least squares regression analysis is an advanced mathematical way to determine if you can make accurate decisions about apparent relationships when the relationship among the variables is statistical rather than exact. (A statistical relationship means that the dependent variable's observed values come from a probability distribution that is a function of other causal variables.) The least squares portion of regression analysis uses statistical standard deviation analysis to evaluate the strength of any correlations found.

You start by gathering a number of observed values, like in the scatter graph. The underlying mathematics quickly grow complex, but there are many computer programs available to do the calculations.

Regression analysis may provide comfort in a computer printout, but it allows for errors. The costs may have been entered incorrectly. Some costs might be left out. Time periods may be mismatched. Finally, it's possible that the correlations, although statistically significant, may be real-world bogus.

Even with all that, least squares regression analysis is a Cadillac of predictive methodologies. The larger your organization, the more likely you will run across it. You would then probably have dedicated cost analysts. Seek out a couple of them and ask them to show you how it works. It will be time well spent.

ment decisions. The second is to get a firm grip on the cost behavior and relationships within overhead and, if you sell or manufacture a product, inventory. It's in overhead that managers first look to cut costs. Inventory is also a good area for finding ways to manage assets better and free up capital.

General Widget Company

All of this might make more sense in context. Let's take a look at a generic widget manufacturer.

We'll start with inventory. The manufacturing process is concerned with three types of inventories, depending on the stage of production: raw materials, work in process, or finished goods inventories. An accounting period starts with a pile of stuff on hand, raw materials. As the manufacturing process proceeds to turn this stuff into things, finished goods, more stuff comes in to replenish the raw materials stockpile. The salespeople are out moving the things into the hands of eager customers. The period ends. There are piles of stuff—some things on the floor in stages of assembly, some things in the warehouse, and some cash or accounts receivables for the things you've sold.

You've also paid out a lot of cash for stuff—warehouses, machines, workers, electricity, etc. You need to know if you can do the same thing again next period. You'll usually have a clear idea during the period about the material and labor costs, but overhead costs are often unknown until sometime after the period closes. You can use a constant overhead factor to estimate overhead costs with a measure of confidence.

Let's toss some figures in here to show the end-to-end cost flow process with beginning and ending inventory balances for a

Raw materials inventory (RMI) beginning balance	$35,000*
Add: purchases	$40,000
Total available	$75,000
Less: production raw materials cost	$55,000
RMI ending balance	$20,000

Work in process (WIP) beginning balance	$25,000*
Add: production costs incurred	
Direct materials	$55,000
Direct labor	$85,000
Factory overhead	$60,000
Total manufacturing cost	$200,000
Less: WIP ending balance	($35,000)
Total cost of goods manufactured	$165,000
Cost of goods produced	$190,000

Inventory and cost flow process (continued on next page)

Finished goods inventory (FGI) beginning balance	$35,000*
Add: cost of goods produced	$190,000
Total goods available for sale	$225,000
Less: cost of goods sold	$160,000
FGI ending balance	$65,000

Inventory and cost flow process (continued)

particular accounting period (* = prior period balances):

The example points to several issues that might draw management attention as potentially correctable. Just-in-time (JIT) inventory procedures might be used to reduce RMI amounts: if the company buys inventory just before it's needed in production, it can avoid sinking capital into excessive RMI. The WIP ending balance has doubled over the prior period, suggesting production efficiency questions. Finally, the FGI has almost doubled. That could mean that the sales department is not converting finished goods into cash fast enough. It could also mean that the company is using its production capacity effectively to stockpile for an anticipated heavy selling season. The accountant's refrain, "It depends," echoes again.

For a mercantile or retail firm, this process is the same, but without the production step. You start with FGI, add things bought during the period, and subtract what was sold; the difference should be what is still on the shelves. With serviceable point-of-sale computer systems available for less than $2,000, almost every retail business can afford to manage its inventory using a perpetual inventory system.

In an automated perpetual inventory system, someone with a scanner records all the stock keeping unit (SKU) barcodes of the widgets as they are delivered. The stock is put on display. As customers buy widgets, another scanner captures the SKU of each item and subtracts it from the balance in the computer. Periodically, you should take a physical inventory of the stock.

Don't Shrink from Shrinkage

Shrinkage is a cost managers will want to watch closely. The **Smart Managing** 2002 National Retail Security Survey conducted by the University of Florida reported that shrinkage rates in 2001 averaged 1.7% of total annual retail sales. The various security devices and tags have cut sharply into shrinkage from shoplifting: 32% of shrinkage is through theft by customers. Sadly, most shrinkage now is through theft by employees—48%. Wise restaurant and bar owners conduct a daily closing inventory. The survey also reported that 15% of shrinkage is the result of administrative errors and 5% is vendor fraud.

Any differences between the figures in the perpetual inventory system and the physical count falls under the general heading of *shrinkage*. The computer

Shrinkage Losses of inventory through breakage, shoplifting, or employee theft. Also known as *inventory shortage*.

count should be updated to reflect the physical count and the difference recorded as a loss.

Inventory Costing Methods

Computers have made inventory tracking both simpler and more accurate, but managers still have to decide how to record inventory costs. To find the cost of goods sold and of inventory on hand, each item must be tied to the actual cost. In this case, GAAP allows four costing methods:

- specific unit
- weighted average
- first-in, first-out (FIFO)
- last-in, first-out (LIFO)

There are industry-specific, tax, accounting, and financial report considerations that guide your choice.

The *specific unit* method values inventories at the individual cost of each unit. This method usually makes sense with higher-priced items, such as autos, jewelry, and airplanes.

The *weighted average* method arrives at the cost of fungible

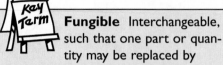

Fungible Interchangeable, such that one part or quantity may be replaced by another, equal part or quantity. Fungible goods can mixed up or replaced with no loss of value or utility. A pound of wheat or nails, a gallon of gasoline—anything that is sold in bulk (by weight or by measure) is a fungible.

goods by dividing the cost of goods available for sale by the number of units available for sale.

The first two inventory cost methods deal with the nature of the inventory. The next two deal with the time period of the inventory.

Under the *first-in, first-out* (FIFO) method, the costs of units placed earliest into inventory are the first costs out to cost of goods sold. Thus, the inventory's asset-carrying value rests on the costs of the latest purchases.

Under the *last-in, first-out* (LIFO) method, the last costs into inventory are the first costs out to cost of goods sold. Ending inventory consists of the oldest costs, those from the beginning inventory and the earliest purchases of the period.

Under both specific unit and weighted average methods, the inventory value does not change. The two period inventories can change in value. The change is usually big enough and the impact on management decisions great enough that serious thought should be given to the choice. Generally, when prices are rising, FIFO ending inventory is higher because it's priced at more recent costs and LIFO ending inventory is lower because it's priced at earlier costs. The difference between gross profit figured on the FIFO basis and gross profit figured on the LIFO basis is known as *inventory profit*. When prices are falling, the situation is reversed: FIFO ending inventory is lower because it's priced at more recent costs and LIFO is higher because it's priced at earlier costs.

Inventory profit The difference between gross profit figured on the FIFO basis and gross profit figured on the LIFO basis. This benefit from holding onto inventory that's increased in value is also known as a *holding gain*.

Comparing the Benefits of LIFO and FIFO

Smart Managing

LIFO best matches the current value of cost of goods sold expense to current revenue, since it uses the most recent costs to purchase that inventory. LIFO users also pay the lowest income tax when prices are rising, because LIFO results in the highest cost of goods sold and the lowest taxable income.

FIFO reports the most current inventory costs on the balance sheet. FIFO results in the lowest tax payments when inventory prices are declining. During periods of inflation, FIFO overstates income by the so-called *inventory profit*.

Under LIFO, the cost of goods sold expense more closely matches the replacement cost of inventory than does FIFO. Managers can use LIFO to manage reported income both up and down. When inventory prices rise rapidly, managers can lower net income and the resulting taxes by buying lots of inventory at year's end, to increase the cost of goods sold expense. If the business is having a bad year, managers can increase reported income by delaying a large purchase of high-cost inventory until the next period, thus delaying an increase in the cost of goods sold expense.

LIFO is an example of an accounting construct that helps explain and manage costs, but is a real-world impossibility. In retail, you want to sell your oldest stock first. It probably has a sell-by date and you could be subject to a fine if you have it on your shelves beyond that date. Because of its artificial nature, LIFO is not allowed in some jurisdictions, including the U.K. and Australia, and discouraged in others, including Hong Kong. Companies that use LIFO must turn to another inventory cost method for inventories in these jurisdictions. In February 2003 the International Accounting Standards Board recommended prohibiting use of LIFO. Most countries permit FIFO and weighted average cost methods.

Which inventory method is better? Since U.S. tax laws make it hard to change the inventory system, the choice requires close analysis. When inflation is high, most companies chose LIFO for the greater flexibility. Other companies chose FIFO since it more closely reflects real-world actions. Still others use whatever is standard in their industry. Companies have different motives for picking an inventory method.

Accounting for Overhead

Managers can find classifying overhead costs challenging. As explained earlier in this chapter, overhead costs are the costs of doing business other than direct materials and direct labor—all those indirect costs that cannot be traced to a single cost object. Costs associated with the personnel or accounting departments, the lubricants and janitorial supplies used in production, the building depreciation—all these costs gather into overhead. Under most cost accounting systems, the first way to divide overhead costs is to split them out among production, selling, and administrative cost centers. *Cost allocation* is the process of assigning indirect costs to multiple cost centers or cost objects, through *cost apportionment.* Those cost objects can include products. For examples, all the indirect costs associated with production—the aforementioned lubricants and janitorial supplies, the janitors and the salaries of the first- and second-level supervisors—could be part of the production overhead.

If the business is fairly small, there may be a single overhead cost with an associated cost multiplier for planning purposes. Larger organizations will have overheads for functions like selling and administrative. You can slice and dice these costs with broad discretion. Depending on the organization's control/compensation system, the overhead allocation process could involve intense negotiations. If managers are held closely to their budgeted overhead allocation figures, they many want a large figure that gives them plenty of room. If they have to use some of their overhead to pay for services from another

> **Key Term**
>
> **Cost allocation** The process by which identifiable cost items, direct or indirect, are charged to cost centers or cost objects.
>
> **Cost apportionment** The division of a cost among cost centers or cost objectives, sometimes proportionally to benefit and sometimes arbitrarily, when it cannot be linked with a center or objective. This involves only indirect costs as overhead apportionment.

The $699.99 Hammer

TRICKS OF THE TRADE

You manufacture and sell two products. Product A sells in a price-competitive market. Product B is manufactured under a cost-plus contract (full cost reimbursement plus an agreed percentage of profit).

You have a large overhead cost pool. To which product would you assign the greater share of costs to increase profits for your firm? Obviously, allocating more costs to Product B will result in more revenue from the cost-plus contract, thereby increasing profits.

After enough $699.99 hammers, the federal government established the Cost Accounting Standards Board to set some cost allocation standards for government contractors. The Office of Management and Budget (OMB) Circular A-21 sets out allowable and unallowable costs for educational institutions, hospitals, and other nonprofits when managing grant money. Despite tightening up in this area, there are still opportunities for abuse.

---

part of the company under some sort of transfer pricing plan, they're likely to want that figure low.

Perhaps the major overhead decision a manager must make is whether to use *absorption* or *variable* costing, which differ only in the treatment of fixed overhead. Absorption costing, which is widely used in financial reporting, assigns overhead costs to the inventory product during the manufacturing process. Under variable costing, the fixed overhead cost is treated as a period cost and is recorded on the income statement as an expense.

Note that the only difference is that the fixed costs for overhead go to the product under "absorption" and to the period under "variable." What difference could that make? (See Figure 6-1.)

Let's look at an example. General Widget's top-of-the-line widget, The Ultimate, has a total vari-

Key Term

Absorption costing
Method of costing that assigns fixed overhead costs to the product as expenses only when a sale occurs. Also known as *full* or *conventional* costing.

Variable costing Method of costing that excludes fixed overhead costs from inventory costs and assigns them to the period in which they are incurred.

Absorption Costing	Costs	Variable Costing
Product ←	Direct materials →	Product
Product ←	Direct labor →	Product
Product ←	Variable manufacturing overhead →	Product
Product ←	Fixed manufacturing overhead →	Period
Period ←	General selling and administrative →	Period

Figure 6-1. Comparison of absorption and variable costing in general

able manufacturing cost of $12 per unit and fixed manufacturing overhead costs of $200,000. GW makes 50,000 Ultimates in a year and sells them for $50 each. This year it sold 40,000. Under absorption costing, the fixed overhead will $4 per Ultimate ($200,000/50,000). If General Widget's management chooses to use variable costing, the $200,000 becomes a period expense. In this case, the variable GSA costs come to $3 per widget and the fixed GSA costs total $125,000. Note that in both cases, the the total dollar amount spent is the same (Figures 6-2 and 6-3).

	Cost of Goods Sold 40,000 Widgets	Ending Inventory 10,000 Widgets	Period Expense	Ending Total (COGM)
Absorption Costing				
Variable mfg ovhd $12	$480,000	$120,000		$600,000
Fixed mfg ovhd $4	$160,000	$40,000		$200,000
Total	$640,000	$160,000		$800,000
Variable Costing				
Variable mfg ovhd $12	$480,000	$120,000		$600,000
Fixed mfg overhead			$200,000	$200,000
Total	$480,000	$120,000	$200,000	$800,000

Figure 6-2. Comparison of absorption and variable costing

General Widget Company, Inc.
December 31, 200_

	Absorption	**Variable**
Account Names	**Account Sums**	**Aggregated Sums and Totals**
Sales Revenues	$2,000,000	$2,000,000
Less COGS	—	—
Beginning Inventory	$800,000	$600,000
Add COGM	$800,000	$600,000
Goods Available for Sale	$160,000	$120,000
Ending Inventory	$640,000	$480,000
Gross Margin	$1,360,000	$1,520,000
Less Variable Cost Overhead		$200,000
Less Selling and Admin Overhead		$1,320,000
Variable	$120,000	$120,000
Fixed	$120,000	$120,000
Operating Income	$1,120,000	$1,080,000

Figure 6-3. Comparison income statement

The main disadvantage of absorption costing is that it creates a tendency to overproduce, because the average cost per unit lowers as more units are produced. If average cost per unit and net income are part of a manager's evaluation, absorption costing will make performance look better.

In the short term, cost of goods sold is lower and net income is higher because some of the fixed costs are left in the ending inventory. Notice that the difference in operating income is the amount of fixed costs absorbed in inventory: $40,000 = 10,000 Ultimates at $4 fixed manufacturing overhead.

One useful corrective for this potential problem is to adopt a just-in-time manufacturing capability. JIT naturally tends to reduce high inventories. Other ways include setting and enforcing a management threshold for inventories, using something besides short-term measures like net income, or going to a variable costing system. Like many management accounting issues, this condition is not necessarily a problem until it becomes acute, tying up capital needed for operations or investment, while leaving a false impression of performance.

Manager's Checklist for Chapter 6

❏ After breakeven, inventory and overhead are the most important cost accounting concepts to master.

❏ Cost accounting is just a way to measure management performance.

❏ Cost behavior patterns in both inventory and overhead have an impact on financial statements that you can control.

❏ In retail there's basically one inventory; in manufacturing there are three.

❏ There are two product-based inventory systems—specific unit and weighted average—and two time period inventory systems—FIFO and LIFO.

❏ Classifying costs correctly and separating fixed and variable from mixed are necessary for valid analysis.

❏ Overhead analysis gives you an opportunity to affect your financial statements also.

Cost Accounting in Action

Conventional thinking would have you add up all the raw material and equipment you bought, all the wages and benefits you paid, and all the rents, interests, and other period costs you owed and then call that your total cost. You would then divide the total cost by the total production to arrive at a cost per unit. The units you sell give you the income to offset those costs. Any inventory left over is just assets waiting to be sold. Simple.

Why the Fuss?

It is simple—as long as the numbers stay low, as in our Liquid Lemons example, and there's no competition. Once the dollar volume goes up and competition enters, knowing the firm's cost structure becomes critical. It drives almost every action you take in planning production, allocating resources, and setting prices.

Many small manufacturing firms start out with a single product and then branch out into more models, sizes, and colors. Management then runs into problems tracking these seemingly

The Overheaded Monster

TRICKS OF THE TRADE Factory overhead embraces an impressive laundry list of costs. These costs can include indirect materials, indirect labor, machinery, maintenance and repair, energy, buildings, depreciation, rent, and insurance. Be sure to add in all other factory costs.

A common myth is that cutting direct labor cost is a key to cost-based competition. For many manufacturers, direct labor makes up only 10% to 20% of total product cost. In contrast, factory overhead costs often amount to 50% or more. Increases in automated production processes increases overhead and decreases direct labor. In the electronics industry, overhead now accounts for 70% to 75% of the valued added to products. In retail banking, computer-controlled systems replace many manual, check-clearing activities.

simple cost flows. There are just too many different direct materials. Overhead suddenly is a real factor.

Cost accounting systems help provide the information managers need to manage and account for these materials. It's still comparatively easy to track the cost of direct materials and labor. Overhead remains the constant problem.

Accounting for factory overhead cost is complicated when compared with accounting for direct material and direct labor cost. Most firms estimate overhead through pooling costs and determining a generic overhead application rate for product cost. Manufacturers do this because it takes close observation to measure the use of each of these overhead costs in each product. These costs are shared. These costs are indi-

Cutting Costs

Smart Managing If you had to reduce total product costs in order to compete, where should you start? Savvy managers know that reducing factory and general selling and administrative overhead yields more bottom-line benefit without crippling capacity to add value. When managers understand cost structures better, they can meet fierce interdepartmental turf struggles with more compelling data. As firms move from labor-intensive manufacturing processes to greater reliance on automation and technology, they're changing the cost geography of both their products and their organization.

rect, which means they do not attach to an individual product. Yet they're factory costs and some method must be established to link them with units produced. If our estimates prove wrong, then our product cost computation is wrong. If our product cost computation is wrong, that may cause us to make many other poor decisions. Accounting for factory overhead cost is one of the more hotly debated questions in cost accounting, because the amount we report as the cost of our products can impact on our firm in so many ways.

The key step in controlling overhead lies in matching overhead costs to the work activities, the cost drivers. While this underlying concept of overhead allocation is not complicated, real-world situations can quickly become data-intensive. In the real world, it can also cost a lot to get and massage the data. The tradeoffs in the need for information and the cost to generate it make finding the most efficient cost accounting system a persistent search. It also helps explain why there are so many systems in the marketplace.

The driving force behind most overhead costs is transactions, not physical volume of production. To understand a transaction, we have to look at the activity or object that is the focus of the transaction. Transaction activities could involve logistics, load balancing, quality assurance, or making changes. Objects might be the factory itself, a product line, an individual product, a batch of product, or a single unit.

In this chapter, we'll look at four specific cost accounting systems in general, descriptive terms:

- job costing
- process costing
- activity-based costing
- standard costing

We will then cover seven more in the next chapter.

Job-Order and Process Costing Systems

Both job-order costing (or job costing) and process costing are

Transaction activity An event involved in the transfer of something of value, such as logistics, load balancing, quality assurance, or making changes.

Logistics Order, execute, and confirm the movement of materials from one location to another.

Load balancing Ensure that the supplies of materials, labor, and capacity equal demand.

Quality assurance Detect, prevent, and correct poor quality in products, including internal and external product failure costs.

Change Update basic manufacturing systems to accommodate engineering changes.

Transaction object An element involved in the transfer of something of value, such as the factory, a product line, an individual product, a batch of product, or a single unit.

Factory Production facilities common to a grouping of products.

Product line A grouping of similar products.

Product A discrete, user-demanded good.

Batch A production order for a specified volume of a particular product.

Unit Individual instance of a product.

absorption cost accounting systems. That means the fixed portion of overhead costs stay with the product until it is sold.

Job-order costing is used in situations where a company offers many different products or services, such as in manufacturing furniture or providing health-care services. In job-order costing, each job is treated as a single unit of output. All relevant costs, including an overhead allocation, stay with that job until it is completed and sold. Examples would be making custom machine tools or boats. A job cost sheet records all the direct materials and labor costs associated with a given job. An overhead allocation is then added.

To calculate the overhead allocation, start by defining the cost objects. Identify and accumulate indirect costs in cost pools. Choose an allocation base—the measure by which you'll assign costs to cost objects. Estimate an application rate. Allocate indirect costs based on use of the allocation base. If actual manufacturing overhead

> **Allocation base** A measure of activity used to assign costs to cost objects. For example, direct labor-hours, machine-hours, or sales dollars.

and applied manufacturing overhead are not equal, a year-end adjustment is required. (We'll look at the procedure for doing this later.)

Process costing is used where product units are homogeneous, such as in refining petroleum, milling flour, or producing cement. In process costing, the total output is treated as a single unit of output. The individual gallon of heating oil or benzene from a refinery does not have identification. Manufacturing overhead is spread equally to each unit produced. As a result of these product/production characteristics, process costing does not differentiate among individual units or specific product batches, other than in the most general periods, such as the production month. Instead, it divides accumulated costs for a period by quantities produced during that period to get average unit costs.

Production can follow process-costing procedures until it reaches a split-off point. The resulting output can then switch over to job-costing procedures as the individual product takes shape. Many permutations are possible during a complicated and branching production process.

Assuming a single product, the indirect costs still go into a cost pool, which becomes the overhead allocation for the unit of production. When there are multiple processes, then managers have to allocate overhead based on their judgment. The criteria for this allocation are as much art as science. One place to start is the product sales mix: allocate the overhead cost pool by the percentage of sales for each product. Different cost accounting systems have other suggestions on how to build this basic analysis.

General Differences

As mentioned, job-order costing is appropriate when there are many different products or services or products that are usually provided on a custom basis, while process costing is used when goods or services are relatively homogeneous. A job-order system focuses on the individual job. The process cost system focuses on the cost center: the cost center's costs are divided by the number of units produced to compute the unit cost.

Process Costing	Job-Order Costing
homogeneous	heterogeneous
mass-produced	batch-produced
small cost per unit	large cost per unit
continuous production	sequential production
uniform production steps	individualized production steps
highly automated	high labor skills

Table 7-1. Comparisons of process costing and job-order costing

Materials and Labor Costs

Under a job-order cost system, specific jobs get their own labor and materials costs. Under a process cost system, labor and materials costs are charged directly to the departments where they are incurred. Process cost systems generally need less clerical work than job cost systems. For example, in a job cost system, a direct laborer can work on several jobs. Tracing each worker's efforts through the job work sheets should total the hours worked. In many service industries, workers have to go to great lengths to charge their hours to various projects.

Factory Overhead Application

Both job-order and process costing use predetermined overhead rates. In job cost systems, each job has its own overhead allocation; that allocation can be anything management finds relevant. In process cost systems, overhead is usually applied to departments. As is the case in job costing, the applicable factory overhead is charged to the service departments. Then the service department expenses are distributed to the production departments.

Product Cost in a Process Cost System

The basic process cost principle charges all manufacturing costs to production departments, either directly or indirectly. In a single-department factory, calculate the unit cost by dividing the total cost by the number of units produced during the period. If there are multiple departments, the situation is more complicated. Products accumulate costs as they pass through each department. Three steps are involved:

1. Service department costs are spread among the production departments.
2. Costs from each prior department carry over to successive departments.
3. Costs of materials, labor, and overhead directly identifiable with a department are charged to the department.

Work-in-Process Inventories

If there's no work-in-process inventory, calculating unit cost is easy: divide production costs incurred by the number of units produced during the period. In the real world, however, there's usually work-in-process at the end of a period. This complicates the cost determination process. Unfinished units cannot cost the same as finished units. They do have to have a cost value because they've used some of the firm's resources. This quandary gave raise to an accounting concept almost as intellectually teasing as LIFO, the concept of *equivalent units.* An equivalent unit is the

> **Equivalent units** The number of completed units that could be produced from the direct materials and conversion costs contained in partially completed units. It's calculated by multiplying the number of partially completed units by their percentage of completion with respect to the costs incurred. Equivalent units are used to allocate costs incurred during the period between completed units and work-in-process units at the end of the period.

value relationship that work-in-process inventory has to the cost of the finished product.

There are three stages of completion:

- units started and finished during the current period
- units started in a prior period and finished during the current period (BI)
- units started in the current period but not finished at the period's end (EI)

Costs must be spread among the units finished during the period and those still in various stages of completion at the end of the period. This usually involves estimating the percentage of completion of the ending work-in-process inventory.

Job-Order Costing

Job-order costing systems are effective when each product or service consumes a different amount of direct material, direct labor, and indirect costs. Jobs that differ in duration, complexity, or input requirements may also call for job-order costing. Costs are accumulated and assigned to the individual products or services.

In a job-order costing system, work orders track different products with varying degrees of labor production time and different amounts of direct materials consumed. Indirect costs are first assigned to departments and then assigned to specific output units. This assignment is often based on a measure such as direct labor hours consumed.

Job-order costing extends beyond manufacturing. Two federal sector examples would include the Federal Bureau of Investigation (FBI) doing specific investigative work for the Department of State or when the National Institutes of Health does a study on the costs of specific medical procedures, such as open-heart surgery

A service provider might use job costing to track the cost of a particular assignment. In this example, indirect costs are assigned to each job based upon the number of direct labor hours spent on the particular job.

Service Industry Production Costs

An unfortunate misconception exists in some service companies, nonprofits, and government agencies that they do not have production costs. People in these entities believe that their service costs are inscrutable to analysis. Therefore, they record their costs only in the most general terms, such as total wages or hours worked.

It's true that a service provider cannot inventory services like a manufacturer inventories finished goods. Still, managers can identify the costs of providing the service just as in a manufacturing environment. Managing and tracking the costs associated with value-chain activities can provide opportunities for improvement. Both job-order and process costing methods can meet an organization's needs.

Managers should analyze activities and cost drivers. An *activity* is any discrete task that an organization undertakes to make or deliver a good or service. A *cost driver* is an activity or event that causes costs to be incurred. Once managers start to see the cost drivers in an activity, they can understand how much value that particular activity brings to the product or service.

Direct labor (400 hours at $30 per hour)	$12,000
Direct materials (supplies, travel)	2,200
Indirect costs (400 hours at $10 per hour)	4,000
Total cost of this specific assignment	$18,200

If the assignment was to investigate a $1,500 charge, the effectiveness of this approach is questionable. Other management methods might have reached similar results at far less cost. Direct labor and material costs flow from certain service activities. Add an overhead factor and it's possible to determine profitability or effectiveness by comparing actual cost with planned cost or perceived benefit.

Process Costing

Since process costing is used for a large volume of similar products that go through the same continuous processes, many routine service activities can use this method. Costs are accumulated and assigned to processing divisions prior to assigning them to products or services. Often costs are assigned to products by dividing the department's total costs by the number of units produced by that department.

Here's an example. A non-profit organization may have a specific department to process memberships and renewals.

Direct labor for membership department	$600,000
Direct materials for membership department	50,000
Indirect costs allocated to membership department	125,000
Total costs for membership department	$775,000
Divided by 65,000 applications processed equals	
Unit cost per check processed	$11.92

This example suggests that both overhead and labor costs need some examination.

As Complex as ABC

Activity-based costing, well known as ABC, grew to offset the distortions in process and job costing systems. ABC is a management practice that looks at how an entity's activities use resources and relate that use to its outputs. ABC breaks down an organization's processes into discrete activities and measures each activity's cost and performance effectiveness. Related activities are assigned costs based on resource use. Then costs are tied to cost objects, such as products or customers, based on use of activities. Any costs that cannot be directly traced to activities or outputs are then assigned to outputs based on a cause-and-effect relationship or through a SWAG cost assignment adjusted through experience.

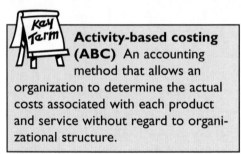

Activity-based costing (ABC) An accounting method that allows an organization to determine the actual costs associated with each product and service without regard to organizational structure.

ABC is popular with many private organizations and several federal sector entities. It lets them designate activities as either

What Is SWAG?

As you may know, SWAG means "scientific wild ass guess." **Smart Managing** And sometimes cost assignments are adjusted for reasons that are not smart. For example, sometimes upper-level managers direct that costs be assigned to departments because they want to make it much harder for lower-level managers to meet performance. Such directives are not strategic, but punitive. So, there are also other factors at play here. The smart manager recognizes that this is the real world and sometimes the people who pull the strings don't do so with the best motives.

value-added or non-value-added. Value-added activities are those activities that cannot be dropped without negatively affecting the quality of the output. Non-value-added activities could be excluded without affecting the quality of the output. Resource costs are assigned to activities. Next, activity costs are assigned to outputs. The costs that cannot be specifically traced to activities or outputs are then allocated as overhead to outputs. This need to justify costs as adding value to a product

Not the Overhead

Non-factory costs are accounted for as period costs. The **MISTAKE PROOFING** firm's product costs do *not* include these fixed and variable costs, as they are not part of the inventory or part of the cost of goods sold. These costs are period expenses. No asset value carries over to a future period. Period costs include the following:

- advertising
- commissions
- sales salaries and wages
- all other selling costs
- administrative salaries and wages
- all other administrative costs
- interest costs
- income taxes

Both process and job-order costing lock fixed costs into inventory. As we've learned, this lowers cost of goods sold and increases income on the income statement while increasing the inventory asset on the balance sheet. Do not compound this distortion like some dot-com companies did. Keep period costs separate.

ABC in Action

The water section of the county utilities department sends monthly bills to county residents, through the finance office. To determine the section's cost per bill (unit), we work with the following figures:

Monthly water bills	$200,000
Direct labor	$50,000
Direct materials	$70,000

The water section bases its indirect expenses on its share of the total utility bills. Assume that the finance office of the utilities department processes 600,000 bills each month and that total indirect expenses are $300,000 monthly. Therefore, the water section adds overhead costs of $100,000. The water section's total monthly cost of $220,000 to process 200,000 bills results in a unit cost of $1.10 per bill.

At first, this looks much like process costing. In traditional government accounting, costs accumulate to object class categories such as salaries and benefits, office supplies, travel, and equipment. With ABC, costs are calculated by activity or process, such as conducting biennial user fee reviews, writing interdepartmental policy guidelines, and, in this case, sending bills.

or service forces many administrative functions to reorient their thinking and performance.

ABC attracts converts because of its many benefits. Managers can improve product costing, because all costs are reviewed regularly to ensure proper linking to cost objectives. ABC helps managers and employees better understand how activities connect to one another and to outputs. Managers can see the full cost of performing and non-performing activities and outputs and then analyze value-added and non-value-added activities.

Better cost information leads to more meaningful performance measures and tools to gauge actual performance. ABC requires a cross-functional look at resource use, so that cost management can blend into other opportunities for business process improvement and reengineering. The closer cost scrutiny can give external parties more reliable cost information through improved financial statements.

> ## Primary vs. Secondary
> Primary activities contribute directly to the central purpose of the department or the organization. Secondary activities support the primary activities. For example, assembling finished products would be a primary activity, while materials handling would be a secondary activity. Administrative functions are secondary activities. It's important to keep in mind that the distinction between primary and secondary is not between direct costs and indirect costs, but between production/service delivery and support.

Implementing ABC

To be effective, ABC has to be set up properly. Otherwise, the result is a mishmash of confused and contradictory procedures. Implementation is a multi-step process that has to start at the beginning and proceed through to the end. The support of senior management is critical, since stopping in mid-process could cause problems.

To start, first identify the cost activities. Focus on defining processes and activities. This task may not be simple. But, like writing good specifications, if this is complete and operationally sensible, downstream steps are much easier. This is the start of determining if an activity adds value or not.

Next, determine the cost of the resources used for each activity. Some allocation may be necessary using the resource drivers—labor, capital, materials, and energy. Allocate secondary activity costs to primary activities as needed.

Then, combine primary activities with similar drivers/behaviors into cost pools based on process, activity level, or consump-

> ## Think Broadly
> In identifying and assigning costs to an activity, you may find using a broader, less specific definition of activities will help kick-start the process. For example, could a pleasant and knowledgeable receptionist who greets callers add value to client acquisition? Wal-Mart greeters suggest that management there thinks so. Recognizing the warp and woof of cost connections challenges you to reach a better understanding of your underlying business processes.

Pattern Recognition

Establishing an ABC system is an outside-the-box exercise.

Identifying and assigning costs to an activity like acquiring new clients can cover a broad range of departments within a company. The goal, remember, is to assign costs to the target activity from wherever sources. Some activities are more closely associated with these objects, such as the business development department, for example. These are the primary activities.

You may want to combine several activities when assigning costs to products. Combining simplifies the system and usually makes little difference in the final cost of objects. The goal is to combine only activities that will result in little difference in final cost, both currently and over time. This means that the activities have consumption ratios in similar proportions by products, both now and in the future.

There is one caveat. Consumption ratios tell us mathematically whether it will make a difference to combine activities based on a sampling of allocations at a point in time. The usage pattern may change over time. We need to look at factors that will assure us that these patterns will hold stable or revisit our assumptions on a regular basis.

tion ratio. Identify a cost driver for the primary activities. Collect information about cost driver usage for cost objects. Take that data and calculate the budgeted cost per unit of the cost driver for each activity. Now, you can allocate costs to cost objects.

Cost objects in ABC can include product lines, individual products, customers, or distribution channels. As with other cost accounting techniques, include any activity you want to manage. Each technique just deals differently with identification, processing, and impact.

To complete the process, add together all of the costs for activities in a pool. Select a single cost driver for the pool. The best choice is the one that is simplest to measure but returns consistent results. Calculate a cost rate by dividing the cost by the cost driver use. Recognize that cost drivers can take several forms:

- transaction drivers—How often does the activity occur?
- duration drivers—How long does the activity last?
- intensity drivers—How complex is the activity?

Cost hierarchy A means of organizing costs into costs pools according to the types of cost drivers (cost allocation bases) or degrees of difficulty in determining cause-and-effect relationships. For example, a hierarchy for production might be as follows:
- output unit level: costs that are applied to each individual unit
- batch level: costs that are applied to groups of production units
- product level: costs that cannot be identified with specific products but are associated with a product family
- facility level: costs that sustain production but cannot be traced to specific products

In looking to assign costs, you should remember the *cost hierarchy*. Costs come in a hierarchy of levels. If you're looking to find the cost of a product line, direct costs will include the following levels: unit, batch, product, and product line. If it's a distribution channel you want to slice and dice, direct costs include the unit, the batch, the customer, and the distribution channel. If it's only a batch cost you seek, direct costs include the unit and the batch. While the hierarchical structure depends on the nature of the individual business, taking it into account will keep your investigations from straying too far afield.

In many situations, an entity adopts a hybrid of two or more of the costing methodologies mentioned above. For example, ABC may be used to assign direct costs and process costing can be used to assign indirect costs.

How to Use ABC Information

The greater clarity that comes from properly implemented ABC helps in several areas. Here's a Top 10 List of the decisions where ABC information can make significant contributions:

- Modifying product mix and pricing.
- Restructuring product pricing and price points.
- Identifying substitute products.
- Eliminating products and resulting excess capacity.
- Improving product design and development.
- Redesigning products.

- Improving production processes.
- Improving customer relationships.
- Changing operating policies and strategy.
- Improving supplier relationships.

ABC will also chop a pound of coleslaw in less than a minute and mow your lawn while you watch television.

Should You Use ABC?

If you want to be a cost commando, ABC offers tempting targets if the organization has large indirect, non-unit-based costs that have grown over time. Another indicator is a large variety in products, customers, or processes. If your organization fits this pattern, you will learn that, without ABC, there's no sunshine. Without ABC:

- Product costs are not fully understood.
- You don't have good cost behavior/cost driver information.
- Some costs are not even tied to products.
- Product costs are not accurate.
- Low-volume products are assigned too little cost; high-volume products are assigned too much cost.
- High-complexity products are assigned too little cost; low-complexity products are assigned too much cost.

Activity-based management (ABM) A discipline that focuses on managing activities to maximize the profit from each activity and improve the value received by the customer. ABM seeks to optimize value-added activities and minimize or eliminate non-value-added activities. ABM includes cost-driver analysis, activity analysis, and performance measurement and uses ABC as its major source of information.

Because of the time and skill ABC requires, it's inappropriate for smaller enterprises. There are also corollaries or extensions of ABC that are worth further examination. One is *activity-based management* (ABM). The key difference between ABC and ABM is that ABM focuses on reengineering and activity selection while ABC focuses on strategic selection of products, customers, and/or distribution channels.

Standard Costing

The most traditional cost system in widespread use is standard costing. Standard costing charges all production costs to cost objects benchmarked to predetermined costs and quantities. These standard costs go into budget templates at the start of a year and are then compared with actual costs during the year. The difference between planned results and actual outcomes is either a favorable or unfavorable variance. Variances drive the feedback loop used in controlling the production processes. Managers then work to conform the process to the standard costing model. It's important to review these standards periodically to keep them up-to-date.

> **Standard costing** A system in which cost components are predetermined using standard costs, assuming normal operations, instead of using actual costs. The standard costs are then compared with actual costs and variances are explained in terms of either price or quantity.

Since compensation and performance standards can depend on controlling variances, standard costing can be a simple but powerful motivating tool. Because its main feature recognizes variations from established norms, it works well with the concept of management by exception.

Standard costing can be used alone or in conjunction with job-order, process, activity-based costing, or other systems. The purpose of standard costing is to have a standard cost per product, which can be viewed as a goal with which actual costs can be compared. Its primary use is to measure the favorable and unfavorable variances between actual and standard costs. Standard costing can be used for such components as direct materials, direct labor, and indirect costs. Standard costing separates factory inputs, materials, labor, and overhead into two component standards, factory prices and factory quantities.

Setting Standards

Standards come from three main sources: experience, theoretical constructs, and practical references.

Experience gives the most realistic standard. Based on what was done in the past, it assumes those circumstances will translate well into the future. Unfortunately, this can lead to a rather cavalier budgeting exercise along the lines of "Take what we did last year, add or subtract 10%, and call it done."

Theoretical constructs are less satisfactory. The ideal standard usually cannot be met. It leads to unfavorable variances as it assumes minimum prices for all costs and optimal usage of all resources at 100% manufacturing capacity.

Practical standards, while often set as an intentional challenge to line management, can usually be reached. These standards should consider at least four things:

- Prices for materials are not always going to be the lowest.
- Labor is not 100% efficient.
- Normal spoilage will occur.
- Operations do not run at 100% capacity over time.

Most businesses presently use practical standards.

You should know that a new manufacturing environment is developing that stresses reaching ideal standards. This emphasis comes because there's too much slack and waste built into practical standards. Management efforts like Total Quality Management (TQM) look to cut this waste. Positive results have convinced some that businesses should now move toward ideal standards. Still, "stress" seems to be the operative word there and the jury is still out on how widely its use will spread.

The unit price standard sets the price at which direct materials should be purchased. Each material needs its own standard. It should be contingent on the sales forecast. Suppliers need to have an estimate of the total quantity to determine the amount of any discount. Also, the company needs to give suppliers the quality and delivery standards before a standard price per unit can be set.

Direct labor price standards usually come straight from a union contract or other negotiations between management and personnel. Any known pay rate increases during the year must figure into the computation. Direct labor efficiency standards can come from union contract work rules or predetermined performance standards for the amount of hours that should go into the production of one finished unit. Any hiring contemplated should consider the learning curve effects: learning curve inefficiency is most noticeable in complex processes that require dexterity, as opposed to processes that are fully automated.

Setting factory overhead standards usually involves input from many departments. Standard costing establishes a single cost per unit, which is applied despite fluctuations in activity. Because of the amount of information, time, and interdepartmental coordination involved, companies that use standard costing often establish a separate department for this task.

Once the standards are in place, management can budget for costs and production. After comparing the budgeted standards with actual performance, management then adjusts operations to track the budget more closely. Also, as noted earlier, management should review the standards periodically to keep them current.

Analyzing Variances

Variance analysis looks at the difference between actual and standard costs. It can measure performance, correct inefficiencies, and deal with any accountability functions.

Variances can be favorable or unfavorable. Favorable variance happens when the actual amount is less than the standard amount. Favorable variances are credits; they reduce production costs. Unfavorable variance occurs when the actual amount is greater than the standard amount. Unfavorable variances are debits; they increase production costs.

Variances come in three main flavors:

- price
- efficiency
- volume

> ### ⚠️ CAUTION!
> ### Favorable and Unfavorable
> Don't be misled by the terms "favorable" and unfavorable." A favorable variance does not necessarily mean good, nor does an unfavorable variance mean bad. Management should analyze all variances to determine the cause. This analysis would include determining if the standard is correct. In reviewing standards, as always, compare costs and benefits.

Factors that can cause price variance include changes in market prices/rates, differences between standard and actual input quality (i.e., higher-quality inputs cost more per unit than lower-quality inputs), changes in delivery channels for materials input, changes in the mix of worker skill levels, outdated standard prices/rates, and random variation in prices/rates.

Efficiency variances can come from more or less efficient usage of materials, greater or lesser worker productivity, direct material quality, difficulty of working with materials, worker productivity and efficiency, less skilled workers, lower wage rates, lower worker productivity and efficiency, inappropriate standards (e.g., ideal standards or outdated standards), and random variation in materials usage and/or worker productivity.

Output variances can accompany any of the causes of price and efficiency variances. In addition, output can be affected when one unit's outputs become another unit's inputs.

Standard Costing Critique

To many managers, standard costing seems out of step with the philosophy of cost management systems and activity-based management. They feel that standard costing puts too much focus on direct labor cost and efficiency, particularly as labor costs tend to become fixed rather than variable. In turn, automated manufacturing processes tend to be more consistent in meeting production specifications.

Individual variances are lumped together in broad categories. Specific product lines and production batches can be overlooked or managers find variances too late to be useful. Flexible budget systems can also be slow. Shorter product life cycles mean that standards are relevant only for a short time and the cost to update standards can grow out of proportion with the benefits. Standard costing's tight focus on cost minimization ignores other significant concerns, like improving product quality or customer service.

Many traditional companies are experimenting with phasing out aspects of standard costing in favor of other cost accounting techniques. Many features can fit comfortably with techniques covered in this chapter and the next. In those companies, standard costing will probably remain as the primary budget-planning tool.

Static and Flexible Budgeting

Budgeting sets clear financial goals for the organization. Budgeting also provides a basis for judging the financial performance of the organization. The types of budgets used by businesses vary somewhat according to the nature of their operations. Here are common types of budgets:

- budgets for sales, purchases, operating expenses, and cost of goods sold
- budgets for cash and capital expenditures
- budgets for production, materials, labor, overhead, and cost of goods manufactured

Businesses usually budget for their fiscal year. The static budget often goes no further than this. However, a

Budget Skills Ranked High

Smart Managing

In a study of employers, the Institute of Management Accountants found that employers think knowledge of the budgeting process is the most important accounting skill for new hires. Managers spend much of their time preparing, defending, managing, or supervising budget activities. If you haven't gotten into budgets already, you might as well start now.

Budgets drive most activities in organizations of all types—new and established, big and small, private and public, government and nonprofit. Whatever their situations, managers need to know budgeting.

year's budget is often broken down into quarterly or monthly segments. This practice makes it possible for management to monitor progress during the year and take corrective action if there are any variances or problems in meeting goals. For an even finer screen of results, managers add a flexible budget capability.

Flexible budgeting is a way to adjust the variance back to standard. Actual prices and actual production rarely match the standard. Flexible budgeting shows what the revenues and expenses that should have been at the actual activity level. Once the standard prices are set, a flexible budget can adjust for any actual output.

Manager's Checklist for Chapter 7

❏ In any cost accounting system, determining overhead is the major effort.

❏ Overhead is the first place to look for cost savings. There will be savings elsewhere, but overhead has the greatest potential—and the most organizational resistance.

❏ Job costing systems fit production runs of products that are heterogeneous, produced in batches, at a high cost per unit, using sequential individualized steps requiring higher labor skills.

❏ Process costing fits production of products that are homogeneous, mass-produced, at a low cost per unit, in one highly automated, continuous production run.

❏ Both job and process costing techniques can apply to services and to nonprofit and government organizations.

❏ Do not include non-factory overhead costs in factory overhead.

❏ Activity-based costing (ABC) can be a challenge to implement properly.

❏ ABC results in better understanding and control of costs. Dramatic results are possible.

❏ Understanding budgeting techniques is a fundamental management skill.

❏ Standard costing techniques let managers set budget targets and then manage from variances from the standard.

❏ Flexible budgets can refine standard costing analysis.

❏ Critiques of standard costing point to an inappropriate emphasis on direct labor costs and efficiency. In addition, cost minimization can ignore important quality issues.

Other Management Accounting Systems

In the Accounting Best Practices Survey of 2003, developed jointly by Ernst & Young and the Institute of Management Accountants, 98% of more than 2,000 senior-level financial executives who participated said their companies do not have accurate cost information. The major distortions come from areas such as overhead allocations and shared services. The executives also wanted more accurate cost information to guide strategic decision-making activities.

They Want It, but They Don't Want It—Yet They Still Need It

One survey goal was to learn what drives management to adopt new accounting tools and initiatives. Not surprisingly, the survey found that decision makers and line managers identify cost management as a key input to decision-making and accurate cost information as the top priority. Information to help in cost-reduction decisions ranked second. Almost 40% of the respondents said that the inaccurate cost information had a "significant" impact on the outcome of their decisions. What was surprising was that 80% placed a medium to low priority on implementing new cost management tools and systems. Spreadsheets and traditional job and process costing still remain the preferred management accounting tools. The survey found that 72% of the respondents used homegrown solutions.

This dichotomy between a strong need for more accurate and comprehensive cost data and a reluctance to implement new tools and systems exists because the cost accounting system lies at the heart of any organization. It probably started in the early days of the company as a glorified checkbook. Management was too preoccupied with more pressing concerns of production and sales to take time out and install a comprehensive management accounting system. As the company grew, undocumented tweaks kept coming to how costs were recorded. Layers of methods and procedures grew along with sales. At some point, the company went to an automated system that meets some needs. Unmet needs wind up being solved through non-integrated procedures. Complicate things by adding that only one or two people might know the formulas that went into the spreadsheet.

Changing such a cost accounting system can require radical and costly alterations to the organization, both psychological and financial. This is why many organizations are extremely reluctant to tinker with their existing cost accounting system. As we saw with the development of activity-based costing in the last chapter, effective implementation requires a series of planned steps with strong management support to bring the organization to a readiness to accept ABC.

Still, the need to understand and control costs is so great, particularly with increasing globalization and competition, that management accounting tools are constantly developed, presented, adopted, and, where successful, refined. Traditional performance measurement focused on financial accounting data starts to become less meaningful as a management-planning tool for growing information age companies. Many of the new tools and concepts now come from business school research or private consultants. Lessons from enterprise-level software packages serving *Fortune* 500 companies are being scaled for small and mid-sized business. At the same time, the management/cost accounting concept has grown to embrace a much wider scope than Andrew Carnegie's fierce concentration on direct labor and materials cost. While the importance of accurate ledger entries for costs will continue indefinitely, how managers examine and interpret those costs is changing at some basic levels.

With change comes a certain amount of turmoil. Some solutions take an umbrella approach and cover everything. Others focus on deficiencies or improvements to current practices. Caution and a clear understanding of requirements are necessary when looking at implementing a new management accounting system. Software companies have provided new packages with attractive capabilities but long and hard implementation cycles. Sometimes companies have just failed,

Development of Management Accounting: Beginnings

Management accounting got a big push in the later 19th century with Andrew Carnegie, who was a demon for knowing and controlling his steel plants' direct costs in labor and materials. Other businesses noted his success and copied him. In addition, the managers directly responsible for production largely developed the cost-accounting metrics. They were principally engineers, not accountants, and took a solutions-based approach. Once accountants got involved, such useful concepts as depreciation and cost of capital crept into decision analysis.

Early in the 20th century, the development of the ROI models such as the Dupont model, discussed earlier, led to a greater emphasis on financial performance. Armies of clerks carried the country through the production boom of the war years and following. The traditional job and process costing systems went through incremental refinements. But the financial model started to show its limitations in the 1980s. (To be continued ....)

unable to sustain growth. They have left many an orphaned company limping along with hard-to-transfer data. Some of the "B" school tools have a "flavor of the month" quality. They flare, fade, and are forgotten. Real-world considerations of internal support and technology capabilities coupled with a clear ROI path should determine which system you chose. As the technology matures, the more stable and useful approaches will emerge.

We are going to look at six management/cost accounting systems that either are getting some traction or have special capabilities of management interest:

- balanced scorecard
- just-in-time inventory

Development of Management Accounting: Recent Changes

In the 1980s, specialized management teams would take over a company, slash direct costs by cutting jobs and selling productive capacity, and dramatically improve financial performance. The company's stock price would rise and all would be jolly for a short while. Then, as the company found it harder to maintain production and quality, market share eroded, the stock price went south, and the managers who had not successfully slipped away were either fired or jailed.

Some well-publicized instances of this phenomenon, such as Sunbeam, helped motivate a reexamination of what made a company successful and how to account for that success. More recently, examples like Enron and WorldCom have shown the costly and shameful doom that waits for those who place their management emphasis solely on financial performance.

Companies are starting to edge away from this financial performance model. Management analysts have found that the most successful companies have a clear set of qualitative guiding beliefs, as opposed to setting quantitative goals such as annual growth targets or earnings per share. The enduring companies always seem to talk about financial and strategic objectives in the context of all the other things they expect to do well. Almost universal among these companies is the idea that profit is a natural byproduct of doing something well, not an end in itself.

- operation costing
- environmental/full cost accounting
- target costing
- transfer pricing

The goal of upper managers is to choose cost management approaches that are compatible with their culture and provide usable outcomes. Companies with significant cost distortion problems that leave millions of dollars on the table each year may benefit by working with an external resource that can perform a high-level review of their management accounting system and recommend an affordable, customized solution.

Balanced Scorecard

By now, who among us has not participated in writing a mission or vision statement for some organization? Done well, it is a bracing and clarifying motivation to action. Done poorly, as too often happens, you just spend precious hours of your life locked in a room with people in love with the sound of their own voices.

The balanced scorecard (BSC) concept, developed by Robert Kaplan, Harvard accounting professor, and David Norton, consulting company president, takes the all-encompassing approach to developing management strategy and turning it into action. BSC builds on some key concepts of previous management ideas such as Total Quality Management (TQM), including customer-defined quality, continuous improvement, employee empowerment, and measurement-based management and feedback. The traditional general ledger system is modified to accommodate these new concerns.

BSC uses feedback—"What's the direct labor cost?"—from internal business process *outputs*, as in TQM and traditional cost accounting. BSC's major innovation is to add a feedback loop around the *outcomes* of business strategies. This *double-loop feedback* process gives managers far greater insight into the effect of their decisions. Suddenly, having the lowest direct labor cost may not be the defining factor if other performance measures are strong.

Feedback Loop

Smart Managing

In traditional manufacturing since about 1920, quality control was a matter of inspection and testing at the end of the production line. The problem with this approach, as pointed out by W. Edwards Deming in the late 1940s, is that it didn't identify the true causes of defects: all you would know is that there was a defect. Deming saw that variations can enter at every step in a production process and that the causes of variation need to be identified and fixed. With that approach, defects go down sharply and product quality can be improved almost indefinitely.

Deming emphasized that all business processes should be part of a system with feedback loops. Managers should monitor the feedback data to determine the causes of variation, find the processes with significant problems, and then fix those processes. This single observation replaced procedures that had been in place for a couple of generations and led to countless more innovations.

Deming is one of the giants of management practice. Study his career and contributions to understanding the behavior of costs and you will be a far more effective manager.

The top managers start to build a BSC from the company's vision and strategies. This is the vision statement portion of BSC. Then, they lay out key success factors. These are the priorities of the strategic plan. Since you can't improve what you can't measure, performance metrics must be developed based on these priorities. Processes are then designed to collect information relevant to these metrics and reduce it to numerical form for storage, display, and analysis. This integration of metrics with vision is a primary feature of BSC.

BSC's next innovation is to force management to evaluate the company from four perspectives:

- innovation/learning
- customer
- business processes
- financial

This step away from relying solely on financial measurements helps establish throughout the company a common understanding of goals. It also becomes the way to account for and measure performance and completes the double feedback loop.

The value of these metrics lies in their ability to give a factual basis for decision-making. Strategic feedback comes from the spread across four perspectives. Diagnostic feedback for individual processes is also available. The feedback from the measurement methods themselves helps indicate which provide useful data. That the vision has been expressed through data also means that quantitative inputs are available for various forecasting and modeling decision support systems. All this can be said to result in *management by fact*.

Some critics maintain that BSC and similar inclusive management systems are nothing more than what good businesses do regularly and you shouldn't have to go through all the froufrou. In one sense they are correct. Successful organizations often come to such practices through trial and error. BSC just lays out the all the dance steps on the floor for you to follow.

TRICKS OF THE TRADE

Quick-Start BSC Checklist

- Start with the vision for each of the four perspectives. Where is the organization going?
- Identify strategies to get you there.
- Define critical success factors. What are you going to have to do well?
- Define how you will measure performance. What metrics will you use?
- Evaluate your scorecard. How do you know you're measuring the right things?
- Create action plans for reporting and operating the scorecard. How do you manage the scorecard? Who should get reports? What should the reports look like?
  - Implement
  - Evaluate
  - Calibrate
  - Execute
- Repeat evaluation and calibration on a regular basis to ensure that you sustain the vision.

Typically, a balanced scorecard has a set of objectives for each perspective and the initiatives needed to reach those objectives. There are targets for each objective and measurements to be taken at specified intervals.

Let's say that the managers place a high value on consistent refresher training and developing advanced skills for the employee learning and growth perspective. Thus, the managers may be reluctant to cut training funds. They feel that better-trained employees will be able to improve their business processes. Improved business processes lead to greater customer satisfaction. Customer satisfaction improves financial results. Improved financial results mean more funds are available for training. Individual managers have performance scorecards based on aspects that they control or influence.

The Learning and Growth Perspective

This perspective includes employee training and corporate cultural attitudes toward both individual and corporate self-

---

BSC Measures

Under BSC, managers use several operational performance measures to replace or supplement standard costs. These measures can include the following:

- Quality control as measured by the percentage of defects
- Material control through inventory lead times or scrap loss
- Inventory control measured by turnover
- Machine performance as a percentage of downtime
- Delivery performance as the percentage of on-time deliveries
- Manufacturing cycle efficiency plus or minus value added time
- Fewer customer returns or warranty claims
- Reducing help desk calls

Some of these might be individual cost control items under other cost accounting systems. With the emphasis of BSC, the objective of reducing help desk calls could lead to initiatives for designing better products, writing clearer instruction manuals, setting up understandable self-help menus for common problems, or graduated training for help desk personnel. This broader search might not happen without the BSC net stretched over all aspects of the business.

improvement. In knowledge organizations, people are the main resource. The current climate of rapid technological change forces knowledge workers into a continuous learning mode.

The 50-year-old programmer may have started out on Basic Assembly Language and IBM 360 OS. Through the years she's added FORTRAN and COBOL. There was a stretch of RPG and then a switch to MS-DOS, BASIC, and Pascal that suddenly accelerated in Windows through C and C++ and blew past HTML. She's currently doing JavaScript Web pages while waiting for the XML class to start.

Management and employees face a strong challenge to keep pace with this level of change. Businesses and government agencies find themselves unable to hire technical workers for the skills new technology demands. Employees are often not offered training because of the expense and the fear that they would leave if they upgraded their skills. Many companies meet their needs through outsourcing with contract programmers through companies in India, Eastern Europe, and Russia. This phenomenon is extending from programmers to many other jobs and professions. An accountant in Calcutta, given the proper software and documentation, can prepare tax returns as effectively as one in Chicago. The BSC manager in Chicago has to make sure the metric performance set stresses using training funds to add value to the accountant's job performance.

Learning and growth form the success foundation for any knowledge-worker organization. It remains to be seen how well the surge to outsourcing will play in the long run. It looks to be effective as long as the companies managing the contract workers pay similar attention to the well-being of their employees.

The growth perspective is not only met through formal classes. It also includes things like mentors and tutors within the organization. How well the organization facilitates cross-communication among employees and with managers can also increase job satisfaction and loyalty. Thus, employee turnover and the cost of training new hires may rank as large metrics for first- and second-level supervisors.

The Business Process Perspective

This perspective is closest to the traditional cost accounting view. It looks at internal business processes. These metrics let managers know how well the business is running. Designing these metrics takes some care, since senior managers want to be sure that they are measuring the extent to which their products and services are meeting customer requirements. In addition to the strategic management process, two kinds of business processes may be identified—mission-oriented processes and support processes. Mission-oriented processes are the core business operation: manufacturing or selling a product or providing services. Support processes are more repetitive and hence easier to measure and benchmark using generic metrics. In this instance, what we are looking at is analogous to one of the costing methods and overhead allocation.

The Customer Perspective

Customer focus and satisfaction measures continue to grow in importance to successful businesses. In some instances, this emphasis has also been extended to vendors. Many cost accounting systems make it routine now to calculate customer acquisition cost and the lifetime value of a customer. Customer satisfaction metrics should include direct feedback from the customer, if at all possible. Ask them how you are doing. If you have given value, they will tell you their level of satisfaction. If the perceived value is low, they may be like the restaurant guest who never returns. Unsatisfied customers will find other suppliers to meet their needs. Poor performance from this perspective is a leading indicator of future decline, no matter how good things look now.

The Financial Perspective

All the newer management accounting systems recognize the need for traditional financial data. Timely and accurate financial statements will always be a priority. This perspective can include other financial-related data, such as risk assessment and cost/benefit data. With BSC, managers should get a clearer understanding of how those numbers translate into real-world performance. The widespread current emphasis on only past financial performance leads to an unbalanced situation with regard to other perspectives.

Benefits

The principal benefit of implementing a balanced scorecard is to align key performance measures with a clear strategy at all levels of the organization using a double feedback loop of internal and external data. Management works from a forward-looking, comprehensive picture of business operations. BSC methodology gives an easily understood common structure that makes personal communications clearer. It also helps people at all levels of the organization understand business goals and strategies.

While your organization may not use BSC, there are certainly several useful concepts that can apply to management activities within a more traditional cost structure.

Hybrid Costing

Hybrid costing is an umbrella term that refers to one or more types of cost accounting systems. It can refer, for example, to the backflush costing procedures associated with just-in-time inventory and to operation costing techniques that are applied when a process costing production run takes on the features of a job order.

Just-in-Time Inventory

In Chapter 6 you had a quick introduction to just-in-time (JIT) inventory management. The basic description of the JIT concept is a system in which each component on a production line is produced immediately as needed for the next step in the production line. JIT is an example of a cost accounting system modification that can be used in conjunction with other, more traditional accounting and production systems.

Traditional production systems tend to be push systems. When one workstation completes a task, the output is either pushed to the next workstation or inventoried. Completion of the task triggers the start of production of the next unit and is not related to what is needed for subsequent stations. Inventory overrun happens if downstream workstations cannot cope with the workload pushed on them. Since managers usually want to get maximum use from production facilities in order to appear efficient, the result often means production of excessive work-in-progress inventory.

In contrast, JIT is a pull system. A workstation gets an order and then requests the needed items for its production from the preceding workstation. In essence, a customer order starts production. The customer can be either the ultimate buyer or another workstation in the production process. A workstation pulls the required items for its production from the preceding workstation. The preceding workstation then withdraws the required items from the work station preceding it to produce the exact quantity needed to replace the withdrawn items, and so on.

JIT attempts to limit work-in-process inventory by enforcing a fixed maximum inventory level between each two production stages. If a worksta-

> ### JIT Results
>
> If your business model will support JIT, there are impressive cost savings available. In one not atypical installation, the company was able to cut the number of vendors by 67%. The restructured production process reduced rework and scrap by 44%. Machine setup times dropped by 47%. The key was that total inventory was cut almost in half, reduced by 46%.
>
> **Smart Managing**

tion's output inventory level is full, it stops production until it gets the next request. JIT production systems can eliminate a large number of non-value-added costs. First, excess inventory costs—the purchase, storage, and carrying costs—are largely eliminated. JIT also cuts down on time-wasting activities, like waiting for output, moving inventory around, machine setup, and inspecting work in process. Production is organized in manufacturing cells with multiskilled workers who can perform a variety of operations and tasks. The ability to understand and substitute for each other allows for wider participation in brainstorming work improvement suggestions. In fact, JIT grew out of TQM management ideas. JIT vendors are selected based on delivery time and quality, since JIT depends on short purchasing cycles and good quality to prevent redos. JIT also gives managers a more direct tracing of costs such as setup costs that were formerly classified as overhead. JIT accounting entries are even designed to cut costs through an approach known as backflush costing.

Backflush Costing Uses

In traditional product costing, costs track sequentially. Transaction recording is timed with the physical sequences of purchases and production. Such a system is expensive to operate and maintain, especially if costs are tracked to individual operations and products, as in job order costing.

JIT production uses an alternative recording method known as backflush costing. This approach delays recording cost data until production is complete. Backflush costing looks to remove non-value-added activities from costing systems. Typically two trigger points are set to record cost data, when raw materials are purchased and when finished goods are either completed or sold. Thus, the cost of tracking work in process disappears.

For many companies, this is a major benefit, since most managers do not find it worthwhile to spend money to track costs through work in process, finished goods, and cost of goods sold that can be captured through other means. This is especially true when production is under statistical process controls.

Think back to the discussion in Chapter 6 of the effects of absorption versus variable costing. In just-in-time production systems, inventory of work in process is typically small compared with the costs of goods produced and sold. Using backflush costing means that when inventories are small, the majority of production costs flow into cost of goods sold and not into inventory accounts. This makes the income statement show a higher COGS and lower revenue while the balance sheet shows lower assets.

Problems with JIT

JIT is a system balanced on a very short straw. Disruptions of inventory delivery for whatever reason can cause significant delays. The risk is largely an opportunity cost in lost revenue and lost production. Backflush costing also yields less comprehensive cost data than conventional cost systems.

Operation Costing Systems

One of the other hybrid cost accounting systems you may encounter, particularly in a manufacturing environment, is called operation costing. As separate activities, job and process costing represent the polar extremes of conventional product costing systems. However, there are manufacturing circumstances that combine the characteristics of both costing systems. Basically, this is useful when a product batch proceeds through a specific sequence of repetitive activities or operations like process costing. Within each operation, each unit of product is treated the same but different materials are required, thus moving it closer to a custom job order.

For example, a production run of men's suits may have basically the same operations, but the material will change from product to product. Let's say three fabrics will be used. While direct labor and overhead, the conversion costs, stay the same, because the process is the same, direct materials costs could change with each fabric.

Typically, you would create separate work-in-process (WIP) entries for each direct materials work order for each operation. You could also trace the direct materials to each batch. You then would create a separate WIP for the conversion costs based on the total units produced. Costs would be transferred as batches moved from one operation to the next until they were finished goods ready for sale. Any over/under applied conversion costs would be closed to COGS or prorated.

Looking at operation costing in relation to other costing systems, we find that it fits along a continuum with job costing and process costing and can be used in combination with actual costing, normal costing, etc. Management makes the system choice and determines if the costs accumulate by job, process, or hybrid system.

Environmental/Full Cost Accounting

One area of management cost accounting that is developing rapidly is known by a couple of names. You will find it called either environmental accounting (EA) or full cost accounting (FCA).

The reason for this growing interest is clear. Environmental compliance costs have reached stunning levels. The cleanup costs in the U.S. alone now approach $1 trillion. These costs are spread across large areas of the economy: from huge petrochemical companies to the corner gas station, from chemical runoff in manufacturing computer chips to disposal costs for used computers, from coal mining to junkyard tires, the costs are everywhere. These costs have been long ignored, but as new regulations, increased stockholder scrutiny, and public awareness converge, they are increasingly harder to ignore. I will refer to the accounting system and procedures that capture these costs as FCA, since recognizing the "full cost" of a business operation strikes me as clearer in intent.

The scale and scope of FCA will depend on a wide sweep of factors. It can be applied to the level of an individual process, a system, a product, a facility, or an entire company. Coverage may include specific costs, avoidable costs, future costs, and/or social external costs. Ideally, an FCA system is layered on a sophisticated cost accounting system that uses many of the features of activity-based costing, TQM, and balanced scorecard.

The first set of decisions must address this scale and scope. How deeply will the need to account for environmental costs penetrate the organization? Will it apply to just a process or will the entire facility/company be affected? Obviously, the greater the scale, the more resources will be required. Other considerations include the nature of the costs. Are these discrete, hidden, contingent, or image costs?

Once the nature of the costs are understood, some environmental costs can be significantly reduced or eliminated as a result of business decisions. Environmental costs, say disposing of waste raw material, may bring added costs but provide no added value to a process, a system, or a product. Environmental costs may also be obscured in gen-

Volatile

CAUTION!

Remediation costs are typically included in nonmanufacturing overhead. Some of these costs are capital; other costs involve permits, monitoring, regulatory, and maintenance activities. Remediation costs are distinguished from manufacturing costs in accounting methodology. Yet, remediation activities directly compete for financial and human resources with production as well as proactive environmental programs, such as pollution prevention. Remediation is consequently related to production decisions through the budgeting process. Thus, inefficient remediation decisions can translate into inefficient production and business decisions. Remediation costs must be properly accounted for and integrated with other costing systems.

Once environmental risks have been identified, the auditor must check for compliance with accounting standards. Several rules governing environmental disclosures have been developed in recent years.

The Environmental Protection Agency has identified thousands of contaminated sites in the U.S. Laws now require responsible parties to pay to clean up their past contamination, which is often expensive. In response to consumer interests and regulatory enforcement, some corporations have had to change their ways of doing things. Some firms have had to learn to recycle, limit waste output (air pollution, water pollution, soil pollution), and, most importantly, follow their hazardous products from creation to final disposal. Consequently, for many organizations, significant risks surround environmental issues. As penalties have increased for poor environmental choices, many companies are paying closer attention to regulations, often going beyond what is required.

In addition, guidance on accounting for several of these items is shifting as regulatory bodies clarify their thinking on these issues. If you run into a situation requiring the application of environmental cost data, check for the latest information on how to handle the situation.

eral overhead accounts and overlooked during the decision-making process. At least that has been the general experience to date. Understanding these costs can lead to more accurate costing and pricing of products. In addition, a competitive advantage with customers may be possible when you have environmentally preferable processes and products.

The major challenge in using FCA as a management tool is identifying relevant costs. The types of environmental costs may be described as conventional, potentially hidden, contingent, and image.

Conventional costs would cover things like material, supplies, structures, and capital costs. These areas need to be examined for environmental impact on decisions.

The *potentially hidden* costs can be some of the trickiest to tease out. Regulatory costs, the fees, licenses, reporting, and mandated training are usually straightforward. The major risk here is that some of the growing regulatory requirements will be overlooked. The major unknown is how high-remediation clean-up costs might go. With experience, the up-front and back-end costs for things like site prep, engineering, installation, closure, and disposal will become easier to estimate. Similarly, voluntary costs related to training, audits, monitoring, and reporting will become clearer.

The *contingent* costs of penalties/fines have generally published ranges. However, there are some potentially crushing fines that would sink any company were the full weight of the law applied. The value and liability of any property would have to be assessed in light of environmental impact. Legal fees to defend or protect against claims have a tendency to be somewhat open-ended. Additionally, contingency factors may require adjustment using the probabilities of environmental incidents, such as spills.

Image costs would apply to developing and explaining your environmental positions with employees, customers, suppliers, regulators, and shareholders. These would be somewhat like advertising and market costs, since it is largely a communications process.

An important consideration about an FCA system is that it must be a flexible tool that will be providing relevant cost data not ordinarily captured in traditional systems. Successful implementation requires up-front understanding of the scale and the scope of application. Once identified, environmental cost information needs to get in front of decision makers and they must consider the data as a component of management's decision-making criteria. FCA systems typically fall into one of three categories—reactive, proactive, and leadership.

Reactive FCA systems will generally spread costs, both capital and expense, across various overhead categories. Environmental costs are typically not assigned to a specific production process or activity. The reactive system usually fails either to indicate that such costs exist or to quantify them with data that's more than sketchy. As a result, it fails to identify cost drivers and minimizes the opportunity to develop tactics to reduce these costs.

Sony Corporation

Sony has a global environmental accounting system to promote effective and efficient use of its resources in protecting the environment. It can monitor environmental preservation expenses throughout a product's life cycle and the extent to which those expenses decrease the environmental impact. (Sony uses a set of environmental indices that measure not only the direct impact of its business activities, but also the impact of its products in use.)

Sony uses FCA to determine the cost of environmental conservation measures implemented during the year and compare the reduction in environmental impact from year to year. Sony has formulated a coefficient to convert the factors involved into monetary values for use as reference. It uses the following categories for its environmental conservation expenses:
- product design and recycling
- manufacturing and service-related activities
- management activities
- research and development activities
- social activities
- environmental remediation

In a *proactive* FCA system, costs are categorized and assigned to specific processes and activities. The costs incurred can be identified, classified, and quantified but are limited to discrete costs. Decisions typically focus on incremental activities, such as minimizing hazardous waste.

A *leadership* FCA system includes both financial and nonfinancial issues in the relevant data used in the business decision process. Systems are designed to include value chain perspectives. Both the process and the product are evaluated for the relationship between inputs and overall value in order to minimize total costs. The data coming from such an FCA tool can satisfy a variety of decision classes, including cost allocation, capital budgeting, and product design and pricing.

Target Costing

Target costing is a set of costing procedures that support a design-to-cost (DTC) approach. Market-driven target prices are the base for establishing a product's target cost.

The target costing concept is similar to the U.S. Department of Defense concept of cost as an independent variable (CAIV) and the price-to-win philosophy used by a number of companies pursuing development under contract deals. This example is included here to show that many costing models exist independent of a company's general ledger.

The following 10 steps are required to install a comprehensive target costing approach within an organization.

Reorient attitudes and culture. The first and most

> **Key Term**
>
> **Target costing** A method to measure the allowable amount of cost that can be incurred on a product and still earn the required profit from that product. The company sets the price of the product just above the cost of manufacturing the product as efficiently as possible. Understanding cost structures is essential to target costing. It also aims at reducing the life-cycle costs of products, by examining ideas for reducing costs in planning, research and development, and prototyping phases of production.

challenging step is to reorient thinking toward market-driven pricing and prioritized customer needs. The more typical emphasis falls on technical requirements as a basis for product development. Most organizations find this sort of thinking to represent a disturbance in the Force. This turns around the more normal condition, where cost results from the design rather than influencing the design. Pricing is then derived from building up an estimate of the cost of manufacturing a product.

Establish a market-driven target price. It's necessary to set a target price that is sensitive to market factors such as the company's standing in the market place (market share), business and market penetration strategy, competition and competitive price response, targeted market niche or price point, and elasticity of demand. If the company is responding to a request for proposal, the target price is based on analysis of the price to win, considering affordability to the customer and competitive analysis.

Determine the target cost. Once the target price is set, the target cost calculation subtracts the standard profit margin, warranty reserves, and any uncontrollable corporate allocations to arrive at a target cost. Any nonrecurring development costs are also subtracted. The target cost figures are allocated among any necessary subsystem assemblies so that each has a target cost.

Balance the target cost with the requirements. Before the target cost is locked in, it must be weighed against product requirements. The best way to control a product's costs is through setting requirements. Determine that the product design at the target market price and that the target production cost will meet the customer's requirements.

Establish a target costing process and a team-based organization. A clear process that blends activities and tasks will support target costing. This process must keep target costs at the forefront of the attention of the entire staff—production, marketing, and sales.

Brainstorm and analyze alternatives. At each stage of the design and production cycle, you have the chance to effect cost savings and design improvements. A thorough review at this stage of the process may clarify those chances.

Establish product cost models to support decision-making. Use these tools to weigh the implications of design changes.

Use tools and methodologies to reduce costs in all phases—design, manufacture, testing, and analysis.

Reduce indirect cost application. About 30%-50% of a product's costs stem from indirect sources. Trim non-value-added costs wherever possible.

Measure the results and keep management focused. Management needs to focus attention of target cost achievement during design reviews and phase-gate reviews to communicate the importance of target costing to the organization.

Following these 10 steps will help you design and produce products that meet requirements at a production cost and market price of your choosing.

Transfer Pricing

Transfer pricing is a cost accounting mechanism to control transactions between profit centers. As companies decentralize operations and push operational decisions down the authority chain, more managers will find themselves in a position to make decisions about whether to engage in transfer pricing activities.

> **Key Term**
>
> **Transfer pricing** The process by which monetary value is placed on the flows of goods and services between profit centers within an organization.

The primary objective of transfer pricing is to reach goal congruence between two or more profit center managers and the company as a whole. In decentralized organizations, profit center autonomy—the degree of decision-making authority granted to a manager—is a secondary objective.

There are several methods for setting a transfer price. Cost-based transfer prices could settle on the variable cost or the full cost of the product. Another option would be to use cost plus a mark-up percentage or just the regular market price. (Generally, market-based transfer prices promote goal congruence in competitive markets, in terms of resource-maximizing decisions.) Finally, the managers could negotiate a price.

An important issue that interacts with the degree of decentralization is mandatory versus voluntary transfers and transfer prices. Does either manager have the option to decline the transaction? In practice, most companies use either full cost or market price when an intermediate market exists.

What are potential drawbacks to using either full cost or market price? When cost-based transfer prices are used, the selling unit generally is the only one with complete cost knowledge and thus may distort such costs in an attempt to control the transfer price. When variable cost is used as the transfer price, the selling unit has the incentive to classify some fixed costs as variable costs. Full cost includes a surrogate for the

---

Taking Undue Credit: True Story

A company president learned about transfer pricing at a seminar. There was an internal unit in the production department that did warranty computer repair work. He directed that all the other departments send their computer repair work to this unit at a transfer price based on the warranty work but that no money was to change hands.

The repair unit dutifully recorded all the repair work at the transfer price rate in the accounting system. There was a fair amount of such work. The president and all the managers were impressed at how well the production unit was doing. At the end of the year, sales for the production unit were up sharply and it was bonus time all around. When it came time to do the taxes, the accountant started wondering why sales were up so dramatically from last year. You guessed it. Recording all those transfer transactions as sales inflated the income. Moral: don't do things halfway.

cost of adding additional capacity (i.e., the allocations of fixed costs to products), but this is relevant only when there is no excess production capacity in the long run. Current market prices may not be good surrogates for opportunity cost, because they may not reflect issues such as timeliness of delivery, product specifications and quality control, and proprietary information about the production function.

Keep at Arm's Length

Many international companies get overly creative in setting transfer prices higher or lower to minimize the impact of taxes. To discourage this transfer price manipulation, governments have established complicated rules based on the arm's length standard. Basically, they require companies to set transfer prices at the level as two unrelated parties would set them if the parties were trading the same product under the same circumstances in a competitive market

International Transfer Pricing

One objective of multinational companies is to minimize worldwide taxes and tariffs. When taxes and tariffs differ among countries in which the firm operates, a company may have an incentive to use transfer pricing to shift taxable income from higher-tax countries to lower-tax countries. In some instances, this can be the sole rationale for opening a branch office.

Manager's Checklist for Chapter 8

❑ 98% of senior executives think they don't get good cost information from their management systems.

❑ 80% of senior executives place a medium or low priority on implementing new cost management tools.

❑ There is a lot of pain in moving to a new management accounting system. Many managers will do all they can to avoid it.

❑ Balanced scorecard is a comprehensive new accounting system that uses insights from business research to give managers a clearer understanding of their cost structure.

❑ One key way that BSC achieves its results is through a double feedback loop of internal and external performance metrics.

❑ Just-in-time inventory is a new, hybrid cost system that applies new cost control insights to the production process.

❑ JIT uses backflush costing to achieve added savings.

❑ Operation costing is another hybrid cost system that gives managers the flexibility to record costs under mixed production methods.

❑ Environmental/full cost accounting recognizes that a wide variety of environmental costs must now be recorded and factored into management decision-making. Getting a jump on full cost accounting can give some companies a competitive advantage.

❑ Target costing is a process that shows how cost data can be developed independent from the general ledger and used to guide decisions.

❑ Transfer pricing is a cost strategy that companies use to transfer goods and services internally within the organization.

Taxation

Since unequal and arbitrary tax policies played a large role in starting the American Revolution, it is no surprise that tax issues still dominate the national discussion. Solutions range from state ownership of all resources and income to no taxes at all. The search for appropriate levels of taxation and its handmaiden, regulation, will continue to energize our political discussion.

For 140 years, federal government financing came mostly through excise and customs taxes. In 1861, an income tax raised funds to finance the Civil War. Hostile voters demanded repeal at the war's end.

Federal financing needs continued to increase. An income tax law passed in 1894 was ruled unconstitutional. In 1909, Congress passed a federal corporate income tax into law. Challenges to that law, combined with rising sentiment for progressive federal action in several areas, led to the ratification of the 16th Amendment in 1913. That amendment sanctioned both federal individual and corporate income taxes.

> ## Beware the Scam
>
> Periodically, scams arise claiming the 16th Amendment was not legally ratified or some other fantastical loophole exists. Therefore, advocates claim, you are not legally bound to pay income taxes. Books tout the claim. Seminars invite you to learn the procedures to follow to avoid paying income tax. Save your money. Eventually, the promoters and their most aggressive followers wind up in jail and/or paying heavy fines.
>
> You can still so arrange your affairs to pay the legal minimum tax. Depending on the nature and complexity of your activities and investments, it can take some planning to execute. While you should exercise due care in legal issues, the tax court often resolves issues of dispute between taxpayers and the Internal Revenue Service (IRS) in favor of the taxpayer. Frivolous or nuisance claims, on the other hand, draw a stern response. Finally, a line exists between legal tax minimization and criminal tax evasion. The difference is about five to 10 years.

As voters demanded more services, creative legislators at both the federal and state levels sought new ways to raise money. The number and kind of taxes exploded. The types of taxes affecting business are now taxes on income, employment, transactions, property, environmental, and excise, to name the major categories. Although it may not be quite as bad as the situation described by Beatle George Harrison in "Taxman"—"If you take a walk, I'll tax your feet"—managers in any business know the impact of taxes.

Adam Smith named four criteria to evaluate the effectiveness of a tax structure. Is the tax borne equally? Is it convenient to collect? Is it a certainty that the tax must be paid? Does the tax harm the overall economy? Tax legislators, administrators, and voters struggle to get this right.

The first consideration is the tax base, the pool of money from which buckets of tax will be collected. Will it be an entire population, businesses in certain industries, or anyone whose name starts with "T"? The next question is to determine the tax rate, that is, how big a bucket will you use? Will the tax be progressive, like an income tax with graduated rates rising higher with incomes, or regressive, like a sales tax, where all pay the same rate, regardless of income and ability to pay?

The U.S. has a largely voluntary tax system. The taxpayers calculate and pay their own taxes. While not unique among nations, such voluntary compliance frees up government resources for other activities. The Internal Revenue Service's reputation for enforcing tax collection actions against several notable scofflaws doubtless encourages such compliance.

Getting taxation rates right is like tending a golden goose laying golden eggs. If you take one egg, the goose isn't too disturbed. If you take too much, you run out of golden goslings. Although incorporated businesses are legally treated as individuals, they cannot vote. Therefore, they are a frequent tax target. Managers cannot afford to ignore the political process when talk turns to taxation and regulation.

Understanding Tax Policy

The federal tax law is a multi-purpose vehicle driven in several directions. Its provisions aim to meet many national goals, including:

- Financial: to generate revenue (the main goal)
- Economic: to regulate the economy and promote certain industries
- Social: to encourage socially desirable behavior

However, there are obstacles that complicate the situation:

- Political: tax law is the end result of a political process; thus, compromises and special interest dealings occur.
- Legal: courts interpret tax law and sometimes cause it to change.

In this climate of sometimes conflicting purposes, the law changes frequently. Tax strategies must be updated regularly basis.

Several proposals seek to change the voluminous, often confusing and contradictory tax code. These include the flat tax, a value-added tax (VAT), and a national sales tax. While each proposal has benefits, there are also drawbacks. In the end, the present situation will probably prevail. It offers too many opportunities for legislators to reward friends and punish foes.

The Principal Taxes
Income

For a C corporation, income tax can be a concern. Other types of corporate entities, the S corporation and limited liability company (LLC), do not pay a separate corporate income tax. These structures are called *pass-through entities*. Any income they earn is passed through to the owners or partners. This income is then taxed according to the individuals' personal tax bracket. Partnerships of all flavors are pass-through entities also. For pass-through entities and individual tax issues, the tax code offers many varied combinations. This discussion will focus on corporate tax concerns.

> **Key Term**
>
> **Pass-through entity** A business structure that is not taxed on income. The business files a tax return, but the income or loss shown on this return is "passed through" to the owners, who report it on their individual tax returns. S corporations, LLCs, and partnerships are pass-through entities. Also known as a *reporting* entity.

> **Tricks of the Trade**
>
> ### Why Tax Matters
>
> Recall the income statement equation balancing debits and credits. The last number subtracted before arriving at net income was the expense item, taxes. If your net profit margin is 5%, it takes $20 in sales to net $1 in profit. Therefore, every dollar in tax expense you can save is the equivalent of $20 in sales. With careful planning, you can have some control over your tax destiny. This is why businesses pay top dollar for good tax advice. A properly planned and executed tax plan can have a large impact on your bottom line.
>
> Under current tax law, the most profitable areas for most businesses to look for tax savings are in the type of business structure chosen, depreciation strategies, and managing accruals and tax credits. That these areas also see a large amount of fraud should caution you to make sure you understand the legal basis for your tax strategy.

The C corporation pays a progressive tax, that is, the tax rate rises as income increases. Like individual taxpayers, all income is taxed, both ordinary and capital gains. Unlike individual taxpayers, capital gains are added to ordinary income and taxed like ordinary income at the firm's marginal tax rate.

States and local jurisdictions may also impose corporate income taxes. In some areas, this local tax takes the form of a gross receipts tax.

Employment

The principal employment tax is Federal Insurance Contributions Act (FICA), a combination deduction to pay Social Security and Medicare benefits. This tax is shared equally by the employer and the employee. The combined rate is 15.3%. The Social Security portion is 12.4%, up to a salary ceiling that adjusts each year for inflation. The Medicare share is 2.9% on all wages.

For each employee, then, the employer pays 6.2% up to the salary ceiling and 1.45% for the total salary. People who are self-employed pay a tax that serves as FICA, at a rate of only 7.65%. However, if self-employed people hire employees, they must pay the employer's FICA share.

The federal unemployment tax, FUTA (Federal

CAUTION!

Yes, You Too Can Lose the Business, Part I

A sure way to lose the business is to not pay income withholding tax. This money is withheld from paychecks to pay the employees' federal and state income tax liability. The legal view is that the employer is holding the employees' money in trust to forward to the federal and state governments. Violating that trust can draw a sharper reaction than tax fraud. This way to run afoul of tax authorities is often combined with failure to pay the FICA tax.

For a manager, the warning signs are when a business is operating too close to the edge of its cash flow needs. Management is tempted to dip into these "trust" funds to get the business through a temporary financing problem. One month rolls into another and soon the warning letters from the tax people turn into summonses.

Unemployment Tax Act), joins with individual states' unemployment taxes. The resulting FUTA/SUTA funds unemployment benefits for eligible people laid off or otherwise terminated. It is a smaller percentage, paid only on the first several thousand in salary. The employer pays this tax.

Transaction

The most common transaction tax is the sales tax. Each state sets its own tax rate and collection policies. Sometimes, localities are also authorized to add a percentage to the state's sales tax. Only a handful of states do not have a sales tax.

"Luxury" taxes are a special type of transaction tax. When government wants to discourage a certain type of economic activity or raise further revenue from a particular class, that activity is deemed a "luxury" and an additional tax applies to its purchase. Automobiles, fur coats, and imported items are frequent targets.

The most recent example of an ill-considered luxury tax was the yacht tax in the early 1990s. An onerous tax on boat purchases spurred a boycott, drove sales sharply down, and resulted in thousands of job layoffs. In this case, it was a couple of golden eggs too many. When the tax was repealed, the industry rebounded.

Other types of transaction taxes include the various fees, stamps, and licenses that may relate to purchase of real estate, motor vehicles, or other major items. These charges may also

---

CAUTION!

Yes, You Too Can Lose the Business, Part II
Another way to lose the business is to fudge on the sales tax collection. State authorities conduct regular sales tax audits. Since sales taxes are a major revenue source, the state tax people are especially anxious to collect.

The first couple of missed payments will only result in some fines, interest, and penalties. Tax authorities prefer that businesses continue to operate and pay off their tax liabilities. Repeat offenses can draw a sterner response. Read the local bankruptcy filings. Some are for failure to pay sales taxes.

be considered user taxes. The money collected often directly funds the agency responsible for regulating the activity. Each state sets its own regulations.

Property

Property taxes are the exclusive jurisdiction of state and local authorities. The biggest property tax is on real estate.

Valuing commercial real estate often calls for more art than science. As a result, the assessment could be significantly skewed from market worth. If the assessment results in a higher tax, it could be beneficial to challenge it through the appeals process.

In addition to real property, businesses often face state and/or local taxes on personal property items used in the business. The business machines, computers, furniture, and all other fixed assets of the business have a tax applied each year of their useful life according to a depreciation schedule. Afterwards, many jurisdictions continue to levy a tax as long as the item remains in service. Over time, a business could easily pay a multiple of the equipment's purchase price in personal property tax.

Environmental

Environmental taxes include the severance tax and pollution control types of tax. Severance taxes apply to industries like

Consider the Tax Impact

Smart Managing Managers often overlook the personal property tax in the decision to buy a piece of equipment. Depending on the equipment and the jurisdiction, the property tax impact could sway a decision from buy to lease to rent to forget.

Another target for management attention, particularly in larger businesses, is the difference between personal property actually in service and personal property charged to the tax rolls. Many businesses forget to delete equipment from the tax property listing after it has been retired from service. An audit of this area often returns a sizeable tax reduction.

mining and drilling. These taxes, covering the act of extraction, make up an important revenue source to states rich in natural resources.

The pollution control taxes are an attempt to overcome the condition known as the "tragedy of the commons." This situation refers to 18th century English village practice of having a plot of land where all could graze their sheep. Invariably, some people would seek to increase the size of their individual flock. The booming sheep population would overgraze the commons, leaving the ground bare. What had been a resource for all was now a resource for none.

Mandated pollution controls like air and water scrubbers combined with noncompliance fines are intended to avoid this condition. Through taxing businesses for the cost of repairing or restoring resources common to all citizens, governments try to avoid environmental destruction. Environmental policy is a still evolving area of tax and regulation. Regulations are a tax or cost applied to business activities. These controls are often associated with extractive industries. Energy production, from coal-fired generating plants to the local gas station, gets a lot of attention. Many manufacturing processes use toxic chemicals whose runoff must be controlled.

Excise

Excise taxes stem from both federal and state actions. These taxes apply against a single item. They are often called "sin" taxes, since they affect things like tobacco, whiskey, and gasoline. Businesses, usually at the point of manufacture, calculate and forward the tax to the appropriate authority. The direct cost to business is only the record keeping and administration. The consumer pays the tax in the final cost of the item.

> **Key Term**
>
> **Excise tax** A tax on the sale or use of specific services or goods other than real estate, such as transportation fuels, telephone service, airline tickets, alcohol, and tobacco.

Miscellaneous

Miscellaneous taxes that can affect a business include tariffs on imported goods, franchise taxes, and occupational taxes.

Corporate Income and Deduction Tax Issues

The general gross income rule for a C corporation is to include all income from any source unless it is specifically excluded under the tax code. The taxable income follows the accrual realization principle of GAAP. Income is recognized (taxed) when realized. Income can be in the form of cash, promises of future cash, or "in-kind" cash equivalents in the form of property or services. "In-kind" receipts are valued at fair market value (FMV) of the property or service. Income cannot be assigned to any other entity.

If corporate assets increase in value over time, the increase is not taxed until the asset is sold. Any income that leads to recovery of the owner/shareholders' capital investment is not taxed. Income is counted over a 12-month period. The corporation can elect a fiscal year as its taxable year if it maintains adequate records. A fiscal year is any consecutive 12-month period ending on the last day of a month other than December, such as July 1 to June 30.

Deductible Business Expenses

To be deductible, expenses must be normal, usual, or customary for others in similar business. A "facts and circumstances" test is to ask if a prudent businessperson would incur the same expense in the conduct of business. Here is how the Internal Revenue Code phrases it (Section 162): "An expense is necessary if the facts and circumstances show it is appropriate and helpful for the development of the taxpayer's business and a prudent business person would incur the same expense." In questionable circumstances, a business can always ask for a private ruling from the IRS on a tax strategy where individual facts and circumstances often prevail. Corporations can also deduct casualty losses from fire, storm, shipwreck, and theft as long as the expense does not represent a new capital investment.

The method of accounting affects when deductions are taken. With cash accounting, expenses are deductible only when paid. With accrual accounting, expenses are deductible when the obligation is incurred.

The IRS code does have some specific restrictions, but even within those restrictions, some discretion is allowed. In general, an expense will be disallowed if it is incurred in an act contrary to public policy. This means payments of penalties, fines, illegal bribes, or kickbacks.

If you are running an illegal business, you can claim expenses just as if the business were legal, unless you are trafficking in controlled substances. In that case, only the cost of goods sold is a deductible business expense. Fines and bribes would still not be deductible. (An exception to this might be parking tickets: even legitimate businesses can claim a deduction if they can show that tickets are a regular occurrence and thus an ordinary expense in their business.) The requirement for illegal businesses to file and pay tax on income is what permits subsequent prosecution for tax evasion. Few illegal businesses file regularly.

Business Bad Debt

Smart Managing

A bad debt deduction is often misapplied. In general, the bad debt must be specifically identified. Some financial institutions can establish a reserve account and use the reserve method. Accrual method accounting permits an allowance for doubtful accounts to estimate bad debt losses. The cash basis business does not have bad debt deduction for unpaid receivables, because no cash has changed hands. Deduct the bad debt as an ordinary loss in the year when debt is partially or wholly worthless.

For example, Tom, accrual method, sells inventory on account for $1,500. Buyer pays $150 down and makes no other payments. Tom has a $1,350 bad debt tax deduction, because he reports $1,500 in income.

Teresa, cash method, performs legal services for $1,500. Client pays $150 down and makes no other payments. Teresa has no bad debt tax deduction, since only $150 changed hands. She reports the $150 in income and pursues satisfaction in small claims court.

Expenses for lobbying and political purposes generally do not meet the deductibility test. There are exceptions for lobbying to influence local legislation and to monitor legislation; those contributions are specifically permitted by law.

Debt vs. Equity Financing

In calculating taxes, corporations may deduct operating expenses and interest expense but not dividends paid. This creates a tax advantage for using debt financing, as the following example will demonstrate.

A firm with 100,000 shares outstanding needs to raise an additional $500,000 in capital. It can do so by selling bonds that pay 6% interest or by issuing 10,000 additional shares at $50/share. The firm pays $3.00 in dividends for each share outstanding.

Debt financing can increase cash flow and EPS and decrease taxes paid. The tax deductibility of interest and other related expenses reduces their actual (after-tax) cost to the profitable firm. The nondeductibility of dividends paid results in double taxation under the corporate form of organization. This relative attractiveness of debt financing can lead corporations to

	Debt Financing	Equity Financing
Net Operating Profit (EBIT)	$1,000,000	$1,000,000
Less: Interest Expense	30,000	—
Earnings Before Taxes	970,000	1,000,000
Less: Taxes (40%)	388,000	400,000
Earnings After Taxes	582,000	600,000
Shares Outstanding	100,000	110,000
Dividends Paid	300,000	330,000
Earnings Available to Common Share Holders	282,000	270,000
Earnings per Share (EPS)	$2.82	$2.45

Table 9-1. Impact of debt vs. equity financing

acquire high debt loads. If business enters a slump, servicing the debt load may place the company at risk of bankruptcy.

Net Operating Losses (NOL)

While no business eagerly seeks losses, one aspect of the tax code takes the sting out of losses. When a corporation records a net operating loss (NOL) in a business year, it can get some relief through tax loss carrybacks and/or carryforwards. The carryback/carryforward feature lets corporations with NOL carry tax losses back to profitable years and/or forward. The number of years eligible for the carryback provision depends on current tax code. The carryforward eligibility lasts for 20 years or until the NOL is made up.

The law states that losses first be carried back, applying them to the earliest year allowable and progressively moving forward until the loss has been fully recovered or the carryforward period has passed. The business can make an irrevocable decision to carry the losses forward and forgo the carryback provision. This election is usually made when a company suffers losses from the start-up phase of operations and has no prior profitable years to fall back on.

Skillful management planning can take advantage of this feature of the tax code.

After a profitable year, management can plan to absorb the expense of expansion or dropping an unprofitable line of business. Losses from trade or business operations, casualty and theft losses, or losses from foreign government confiscations can create a NOL.

When there are NOLs from two or more years, use them on a FIFO basis. For a carryback NOL, the business must recompute taxable income and the income tax due, if any, on the revised profit figure. Based on the new calculation, the business can choose to have excess tax paid on the old profit figure refunded or applied to future tax obligations.

The recalculation can be involved. For example, limitations and deductions based on adjusted gross income (AGI) and any tax credits based on taxes paid must be recomputed.

If excess NOL remains after applying the carryback calculation, any remaining NOL is then carried forward. After using the NOL in the initial carryover year, the business must determine how much NOL remains to carry to future years.

Cost Recovery and Depreciation

When a firm buys a business or income-producing asset, the cost has to show up on the books as an expense. A variety of methods have developed to account for this cost recovery. For fixed assets, cost recovery comes through one of the depreciation methods. Intangible assets follow amortization schedules. Natural resource cost recovery falls under depletion tables. Intangible assets and resource depletion are areas for specialized study.

The concept of depreciation reflects the accrual accounting method. This assumes that the economic life of an asset will be consumed over time so a portion of its cost must be charged to each time period. The IRS mandates the use of the modified accelerated cost recovery system (MACRS) in calculating depreciation for tax purposes. A variety of other depreciation methods are often used for financial reporting purposes. These depreciation methods include double declining balance, sum-of-the-years, and straight line.

Under the basic MACRS procedures, the depreciable value of an asset is its full cost, including outlays for installation. There is no adjustment for expected salvage value as there is under some other depreciation methods. MACRS has several property class-

---

Key Term

Modified accelerated cost recovery system (MACRS) A depreciation method for writing off over time the value of depreciable property other than real estate, introduced by the Tax Reform Act of 1986. As the name states, MACRS is a series of modifications to the accelerated cost recovery system (ACRS). With MACRS, businesses write off the costs of qualified property over predetermined periods, which allows faster recovery of costs than straight-line depreciation. MACRS is mandatory for most depreciable assets placed in service after December 31, 1986.

MACRS Depreciation

Erskine Corporation bought and installed a machine with a five-year MACRS recovery period. The cost was $50,000. Using the applicable MACRS rates, the depreciation expenses are as shown below.

Year	MACRS Rate	Depreciation
1	20%	$10,000
2	32%	$16,000
3	19%	$9,500
4	12%	$6,000
5	12%	$6,000
6	5%	$2,500
Totals	100%	$50,000

es and life spans. Fit the property to the class and you have the predetermined depreciable life span and annual percentages. MACRS also has conventions for determining when property was placed in service during a year.

As long as you have positive taxable income, you would always prefer to expense any asset purchase. Remember: a dollar saved today is worth more than a dollar saved tomorrow. The ideal depreciation schedule would be to expense 100% of all asset purchases in the year placed in service. Many small businesses have something like that through the provisions of Section 179 of the tax code.

Under Section 179, a business can elect to immediately expense a specific amount of tangible asset purchases up to a statute limit. That limit changes every year based on inflation and other tax policy considerations. To make certain that the benefit applies only to small business, there is also an upper limit on asset purchases. Above that limit, there is a one-for-one dollar reduction until any Section 179 benefit is exhausted. Section179 cannot be used to buy real estate or income-producing property. The deduction cannot exceed taxable income

Section 179

For the year, assume the Section 179 deduction limit is $25,000 and the maximum asset purchase amount is $230,000. If Erskine Corporation purchases assets worth $25,000 during the year, it can expense the entire amount against income. If Erskine purchases $50,000 in assets, it can expense $25,000 and depreciate $25,000 under MACRS rules for the asset class. If it spends $250,000 on fixed assets, its Section 179 deduction is limited to $5,000 ($250,000 - $230,000 = $20,000, $25,000 − $20,000 = $5,000). If Erskine spends $1 more than $255,000, no Section 179 deduction is allowed. Cost recovery will then be straight MACRS depreciation.

before Section 179 is applied.

Financial managers are traditionally more concerned with cash flows rather than profits as the basic measure of business health. To adjust the income statement to show cash flows from operations, all noncash charges should be added back to net profit after taxes. By lowering taxable income, depreciation and other noncash expenses create a tax shield and enhance cash flow.

Hybrid Tax Accounting

In the Chapter 2 discussion of GAAP, we went into the cash and accrual methods of accounting. The IRS permits for tax purposes a third type of accounting method, called hybrid. Hybrid combines cash and accrual methods. When inventory is a material income-producing factor, hybrid offers some tax advantages. It uses the accrual method for calculating gross profit (i.e.,

Hybrid method An accounting method allowed by the IRS for tax purposes, combining cash and accrual methods. It uses the accrual method for calculating gross profit and the cash method for remaining income and expenses.

sales - cost of goods sold) and the cash method for remaining income and expenses.

Alternative Minimum Tax (AMT)

The Alternative Minimum Tax (AMT) is separate but parallel income tax system. The intent behind it was that no one could escape a tax liability through manipulating credits and deductions. The AMT computation reconciles taxable income through adjustments and preferences with the Alternative Minimum Taxable Income (AMTI). If the AMT exceeds the liability computed using the regular method, a business pays the AMT, calculated at a flat 20% rate. Income levels have risen while the AMT legislation remains largely unchanged, so more and more businesses and individuals are falling subject to it.

Tax Credits

Tax credits reduce a corporation's tax liability. They serve as incentives to promote certain business activities. There are two kinds of tax credits, refundable and nonrefundable. Refundable credits can be used even if the tax liability is less than the amount of the credit. Nonrefundable credits can be used only to offset any tax liability. If the credit exceeds the tax liability, the excess is lost. A few nonrefundable credits have carryover provisions for excess. Most business-related tax credits are nonrefundable.

A number of business credits are combined into one amount, called the *general business credit*. The energy credit chops off 10% of expenditures on solar energy and geothermal property. The research activities credit has two parts, a basic research credit and an incremental research activities credit; both credits are a percentage of qualified research and development expenditures in excess of specified base amounts. The foreign tax credit applies to both individuals and corporations that pay foreign income taxes. Instead of claiming a credit, a corporation can claim a deduction for the taxes paid on foreign income, up to a statutory limit.

There are often credits promoting employment or employment within certain localities identified by the Small Business Administration. The welfare-to-work credit applies to first 24 months of wages paid to individuals who have been long-term recipients of family assistance welfare benefits. Individual states may offer credits as well.

Housing and real estate have several attractive credits. The low-income housing credit is issued on a nationwide allocation program to qualified development projects that rent units to low-income tenants. The rehabilitation expenditure credit is a percentage of expenditures made to substantially rehabilitate industrial and commercial buildings and certified historic structures. Small businesses can qualify for the disabled access credit to defray costs incurred in complying with the Americans with Disabilities Act.

Tax Practice

Given that taxes are complicated and this overview of taxes is brief, you may want to consider a tax advisor. For most W-2 wage earners grossing less than $100,000 a year, with no stock or real estate investments, any of the inexpensive tax software packages should be adequate. For business owners and higher wage earners, some tax advice will likely pay for itself several times over. Having a knowledgeable person guide you through the thickets of tax code prose to help point out deductions to take or pitfalls to avoid can be valuable.

Unfortunately, there is a downside: the area of tax practice is largely unregulated. Professionals like CPAs and attorneys must follow certain ethical standards. For example, ethical guidelines issued by the American Institute of Certified Public Accountants (AICPA) instruct CPAs not to take a questionable position on client's tax return in hope of it not being audited. Other instructions include using reasonable client estimates and answering every question on the tax return, even if disadvantageous to client. Also, CPAs will ask to review two or three prior year

> ### Enrolled Agents
> **TRICKS OF THE TRADE**
>
> Enrolled agents (EAs) are a well-kept secret. EAs are individuals licensed by the federal government to represent taxpayers before the IRS. These tax advisors either have had at least five years' relevant service with the IRS or have passed a comprehensive two-day certification test on the tax code. In contrast, the two-day CPA examination has only a portion dedicated to tax questions. Also, some EAs also have a business accounting background.
>
> There are state EA associations that keep a list of EA members available for referral. To find an EA, visit the Web site of the National Association of Enrolled Agents, www.naea.org.

returns. If they discover an error in a prior year tax return, they will advise the client to correct the return. This review service can often result in a refund, since individual preparers often overlook deductions.

The IRS can impose various penalties against preparers who violate prescribed acts and procedures. Statutory penalties may be levied on tax return preparers for procedural failures such as not providing a copy of the return to the taxpayer, not signing the return as preparer, and not keeping copies of returns. More severe penalties await tax return preparers who understate tax liability based on an unrealistic position, willfully attempt to understate tax, or fail to exercise due diligence in determining eligibility for the earned income credit or the amount.

The IRS has recently made strong and positive steps to improve its manuals, forms, procedures, and customer service. The tax code is now simpler in terms of the more straightforward individual taxpayer issues. For businesses, though, tax matters still need close attention. When you weigh the dollar saved in taxes against the multiples of effort to earn a dollar in sales, managing affairs so as to pay the legal minimum tax makes good business sense.

Manager's Checklist for Chapter 9

❑ The tax code evolved to serve goals other than just revenue generation.

❑ The principal taxes a business must consider include income, employment, transaction, property, environmental, and excise.

❑ All corporate income from all sources is subject to tax.

❑ Deductions can come from ordinary business expenses and application of tax planning strategy in areas of corporate financing, managing losses, and depreciation.

❑ Certain business operations may be eligible for tax credits.

❑ Select a proper tax advisor.

❑ Closer attention to tax issues can have a large bottom-line payoff.

Advanced Fraud

In Chapter 2, you had a chance to learn some of the ways corporate managers can influence a company's financial statements. You saw that when and how revenue was booked could move income up or down. Extending depreciation was another income-enhancing tactic. You also saw how these maneuvers did not conform to GAAP. In fact, members of the public, legislators, journalists, prosecutors, and more than a few jurors have decided that these actions constitute fraud. Considering the global impact of WorldCom and Enron and the Sarbanes-Oxley Act of 2002, a basic understanding of what sorts of fraud a manager might run across could prove useful.

This chapter will give a wide sweep of both external and internal fraud. It will show how a manager has to anticipate fraud at almost every turn, but not turn into a quivering paranoid.

Fraud—Here, There, and Everywhere

First, we have to recognize an ugly truth. The reason there is so much fraud in business, as in all areas of society from corked bats to cooked books, is that it works—sometimes. If you steal $50 million, chances are you'll get to keep 15%-20% of it after the taxes, the lawyer's fees, the fines, and about two years— maybe five, if they're really mad at you—at Club Fed. If you don't mind doing the perp walk for the media with a couple of deputies at your elbows, if you don't mind your kids knowing that you took money away from their friends' parents and grandparents, if you don't mind that colleagues cannot find work because of their association with you—if you don't mind any of that, you're probably enough of an amoral sociopath to give it a shot.

You're going to run across fraud in your managerial life. You'll recognize it because that's when some person or organization willfully makes an *untrue* representation about an *important* fact or event to you or your organization. You believe it. You rely on it. You act on it. And you lose money or property as result of relying on their false representation. The fraud's gains can be either direct or indirect, money, property, a job promotion ....

Top 10 Frauds

This is a brief guide to understanding fraud—if you don't already.

Bribery is giving, receiving, offering, or soliciting anything of value in order to influence a person in the imperfect performance of their duties.

Illegal gratuity is giving, receiving, offering, or soliciting, after the fact, anything of value for or because of the perfect or imperfect execution of an official act.

Conflict of interest is when a person has a hidden bias or self-interest that would adversely affect someone else and acts on that bias to cause that person a loss.

False statements/claim occur when someone knowingly makes a false statement or claim that results in economic loss to the recipient of the statement or claim.

Extortion is when a person gets something from someone under threat of force.

Conspiracy before/after occurs when two or more people agree to commit a crime and at least one of them does so.

Embezzlement happens when a person in a trust relationship takes property whose access stems from the trust relationship.

Mail/wire fraud is, under U.S. law, the use of a telephone or the postal service in any fraudulent activity.

Failure to report a felony to law enforcement authorities should be obvious: if someone knows that a fraud has been committed, fails to report it, and then actively engages in concealing the fraudulent act or evidence, it's a felony. Concealing fraud includes acts like changing, hiding, or destroying official records.

Breach of fiduciary duty occurs when a person who's under an obligation to exercise his or her discretion and expertise in the best interest of another party betrays that trust and confidence by doing something that is not in the best interest of that party. Breach of fiduciary duty is a civil offense, not criminal, so the proof required is simpler than for criminal fraud and it's not necessary to prove wrongful intent.

All the above examples of bribery, illegal gratuities, fraudulent conflict of interest, and making false statements are felony crimes. They are also breaches of fiduciary duty. This means that the persons who have committed wrongful acts can be sued for damages in civil court.

Someone might go persnickety legalistic on you and claim that when you give doughnuts to the police who eat lunch in your restaurant it constitutes offering a bribe and that the officers who accept them are guilty of seeking an illegal gratuity. That's a bit too narrow. It seems to me that the two main considerations are the intent and the degree of any financial or material loss incurred. When do activities cross over a line from acceptable forms of business behavior to actions that might involve legal liability?

If we are grown up enough to know that fraud is an unfortunate daily occurrence, we should be armored enough to recognize it when it appears. For example, does anyone really expect that the good doctor in the Oil Ministry of Nigeria is going to give you 30% of the $27,833,672.04 that is the estate of the late son of the former dictator if you will just help him take care of some touchy interbank transfer of funds using your credit card account?

That you can handle easily. The test comes when a coworker plops down next to you and says, "Sales are really down this quarter, but I know a way you can help us all hit bonus level. Just tune the line up a bit so we end the quarter with enough excess inventory to make our balance sheet numbers." What do you do?

Sarbanes-Oxley Act

While it's still unclear whether the Sarbanes-Oxley Act, signed into law July 30, 2002, will eliminate fraud, we do know that it's causing changes. Two major ones make executives more accountable for SEC disclosures and block CPA firms from performing non-audit services for their audit clients.

Sarbanes-Oxley in Brief

Smart Managing   The Sarbanes-Oxley Act is the most important piece of legislation affecting corporate governance, financial disclosure, and public accounting since the early 1930s.

It established the Public Company Accounting Oversight Board to regulate corporate auditors, taking that responsibility away from the accountants. The board consists of five members appointed by the Securities and Exchange Commission (SEC) and subject to oversight by the SEC. The board is responsible for registering public accounting firms that prepare audit reports. It also establishes or adopts standards for auditing, quality control, ethics, and independence. In addition, it inspects, investigates, and disciplines public accounting firms and enforces compliance with the act.

The Sarbanes-Oxley Act also requires CFOs and CEOs to take responsibility for the financial statements (Forms 10-K and 10-Q) of their companies. They must certify that they each have reviewed the statements, that they make no false material statements and do not omit any material facts, and that they fairly present the financial state of the companies.

Sarbanes-Oxley, known colloquially as SarbOx or Sarbox, established new rules, from audit committee members to penalties for cheating corporate chieftains, up to $5 million in fines and 20 years in prison. Directors are facing up to their new responsibilities. CEOs and their teams are now starting to comprehend a new set of rules and put into place new policies and procedures. The big companies at which it was aimed are in statutory compliance.

Under Section 404, companies will add to their annual reports an "internal control report" attesting to the effectiveness of financial reporting procedures. Both management and an outside auditor will have to certify the report.

SarbOx has already given rise to some new C-level jobs, such as Corporate Compliance Officer (CCO). The CCO regulations state that companies not only have to certify their financials but must also confirm their internal control infrastructure. Since internal controls are the focus, many companies are taking the time to analyze and simplify their internal processes. SarbOx amplifies the benefits from workflow automation. Once a process is automated, it's easier to certify. However, it's unlikely that SarbOx, by itself, will bring about the change in ethical outlook needed to turn show-and-sell into fun with numbers.

Employment Trust Fund Fraud

It seems like there is no tax that's not worthy of a concentrated try to evade it. For small businesses, one of the more prevalent high-dollar frauds stems from the employer failing to make all the required FICA trust fund deposits. In the U.S., Social Security is funded by a 12.4% tax on salaries up to a designated ceiling that changes each year. Medicare gets 2.9% of each salary dollar up to the salary top itself. The employer and employee share equally in the resulting 15.3% tax. In addition, the employer is obliged to withhold an estimated income tax from each paycheck. This amount could fall between 10% and 30%. If we assume your payroll is $300,000 and we use 20% as the effective tax rate, that results in total withholding and FICA/Medicare payments of $105,900 ($300000 x15.3% + $300000 x 20%). In addition, in states with an income tax, smaller sums would be involved, based on each state's tax rates.

Depending on total salary levels, the federal/state deposits are made monthly or quarterly. The business then submits a quarterly report. If the business is large enough, this report can go in electronically. Federal and state governments receive a predictable cash flow each month and roughly enough money is withheld for each employee to meet his or her filing obligation. There are also federal and state unemployment insurance forms to file and taxes to pay. Generally, when a business has problems in one of these areas, it has problems in all of them.

Now, here's the sad part. Most businesses do not intend to stiff their employees. What happens in the course of business operations is that some need springs up that only cash right now can solve. The money that was set aside to pay the withholding suddenly looks quite attractive. The employer takes the money, rationalizing that it can always be replaced from next week's receipts. When the time rolls around to pay the withholdings into their respective trust funds, the till is short, so no money is paid in. The employer may or may not file the required forms telling the IRS and the state how much money they should be getting.

This condition can go on for a couple of years with the federal and state tax offices sending out escalating letters requesting payment. Then the tax inspectors start calling. The first calls usually come from the state tax authorities. Their only interest is the state withholding, but their cash needs are generally greater and their collection interest is higher.

Now the authorities have to make a decision: are they dealing with a business struggling at the margins with poor management control and little understanding of the tax process or are they dealing with a scofflaw who is pocketing the money?

If the answer is the former, the employer will have to pay a fine and some penalties, usually, and agree to a plan to pay its liabilities. If the answer is the latter, expect a swift shutdown of the business and a forced sale of its assets to meet the tax obligation. Most of the monthly bankruptcy business sales that you see are assets on the block to satisfy tax bills.

The reason authorities can take such drastic action is that they consider the withholding monies to be *trust* funds. The governments let employers hold those funds in trust on their pledge to turn them over at the specified times. Since part of money is destined for Social Security and Medicare benefits for workers and their families under the Federal Insurance Contributions Act (FICA), the taxing authorities place a high premium on collecting on these obligations. Social Security taxes pay for benefits under the old age, survivors, and disability insurance part of FICA and Medicare taxes pay for hospital benefits.

The typical criminal manifestation of this activity is in either a restaurant or a small construction company that the owner operates for a couple of years and then leaves. A twist is when the crook recruits some people to collaborate in a scam. The crook sets up a shell company and fills 941 and W-2 withholding reports claiming high salaries. When the associates file their tax returns, they split the refunds with the crook. Of course, the authorities show up a bit later and things get unpleasant for the marks.

While Social Security and Medicare are certainly not without problems, the fraudulent employer, by not depositing the necessary trust funds, could also be denying those employees FICA coverage. The employees are still liable for the withholding and income tax on their salaries and payment for their portion of the FICA contribution. In effect, they will lose about double, the money withheld but never paid and the money paid to meet their tax obligation.

When the IRS pursues a criminal investigation concerning employment tax evasion, it wins about 80% of the time. The jail terms run a bit under two years and there's usually a fine for the back taxes. The states do a lot of work also. Check out the monthly bankruptcy filings in the business pages; most are for back taxes, employment and/or sales.

Other Employment Tax Evasion Schemes
Here are some of the other more prevalent wrinkles for evading employment taxes.

Pyramiding employment taxes is when a business withholds taxes from its employees but intentionally fails to pay them to the IRS and the state. Bankruptcy is a way out for the pyramiding masters. That way, they can discharge accrued liabilities and then start a new business with a new name and do it all over again.

Employee leasing is legal but it can be abused. A company contracts with a firm to handle all administrative, personnel, and payroll services for its employees, who are then considered leased to the company. The employee-leasing firm then defaults on paying employment and/or withholding taxes to the IRS or the state. Suddenly, poof! The firm disappears, leaving unpaid employment taxes and unhappy clients and employees.

Paying employees in cash is a common way of evading income and employment taxes. This is a particularly attractive option for young employees. The government loses tax revenue, of course, but the greater loss could be to the employees, whose future Social Security or Medicare benefits are reduced.

With **failing to file payroll tax returns** or **filing false payroll tax returns**, the company just fails to file employment tax returns or understates wages when it files returns so it pays a lower tax.

External Fraud

While you're looking for fraud situations within the business operation, there's an external fraud lurking that could well sink your business—credit cards. If your business takes credit cards, you may find that credit card chargebacks can be serious enough to sink you.

So, the trick is to avoid credit card fraud. First, all card issuers now have premium software that can help in recognizing fraud patterns. Today, most online fraud comes from one of four groups— friendly, opportunistic, organized, and internal.

The *friendly* fraud happens when a legitimate cardholder lends the card to a friend to order something and says it never arrived. The merchant still suffers the chargeback. The *oppor-*

tunistic fraud happens when someone finds a card or some valid payment information and uses it to joyride. This is the kind of threshold experience that could lead the beneficiary to make more organized attempts. I once stupidly left a card at a service station, in a pump reader. I paid for about four fill-ups before I got the card cancelled. The individual wisely didn't try to use the card at anything but the most anonymous card transaction.

Then there's the *organized* fraud by rings of criminals using sophisticated

Chargeback A reversal against a sale that was credited to a merchant's account, resulting in the debiting of the amount of the transaction. The merchant loses in several ways: the inventory is lost, the purchase price is lost, there are fees charged for each chargeback, and a merchant can lose the account if the number of chargebacks is excessive.

How to Lose Hundreds of Pounds Fast

I was shocked when I opened my American Express bill about 10 years ago and found a $15,000 charge on it made from England. Some good British merchant had to eat that bill. Most small businesses would find that hard to swallow. It's estimated that $1.8 billion will be lost to credit card fraud this year.

equipment and identity theft. Largely based outside the U.S., they move quickly to escape detection. They're the biggest single threat to credit card transaction. As in every fraud scenario, there is always the risk of *internal* collusion. Employees of companies with secured cardholder data on file may get access to valid payment data. They might also reveal information about the latest defensive techniques.

There are some well-known and commonly used tips to protect your credit card sales activities. Two quick clues are high-volume, high-value orders. An order for two dozen $200 tennis shoes in multiple sizes should probably raise an eyebrow. If this comes from a first-time buyer in one of the global fraud hot spots—Indonesia, Nigeria, or Eastern Europe—and uses one of the free e-mail addresses, that might nudge the other eyebrow up. If the order asks for a rush shipment to multiple addresses, then it might be time to blow the whistle.

You can also ask customers for the CVC2 (MC), CVV2 (Visa), and CID (AMEX) verification numbers. Visa reports that this alone will cut chargebacks by 26%. Let the customer know what name will show on statements as the charging company. Too many charges have been refused because people did not associate the purchase with that company name. (That's a misunderstanding and not technically fraud—but it still costs!)

Require signatures on delivery. Use a carrier that requires a signature on delivery and lets you keep a copy of the signature. Retain these for your records. As some further protection at the point of sale, you can ask for copies of the identification and credit card. The more you can show that you are serious about identifying your customers, the more likely the fraudsters will get chilly feet and bolt.

Finally, post a warning message on the order page of your Web site. Say that IP addresses are being logged and that anyone who tries to place a fraudulent order will be identified through his or her IP address. That measure will greatly reduce the number of instances of fraud.

Beginning Finance

The Association of Certified Fraud Examiners study mentioned earlier found that small businesses seeking financing from private individuals were most likely to present fraudulent financial statements. An unfortunate percentage seems to come from ignorance of financing operations and how to get business financing.

Businesses have several financing options. The well-worn path is a working capital credit line from a bank: this credit agreement lets the business draw cash as needed to pay current bills while waiting to collect on its outstanding accounts. Banks offer a wide variety of terms and combinations of lines of credit and installment loans. The common denominator is that all loans depend on the business's credit rating, which is based in large part on its financial statements. Recall from Chapter 4 that financial ratio analysis is often a determining factor in credit ratings.

The temptation to present the best financial picture for your business may lead to some of the exaggerations and misstatements discussed in Chapter 2, such as booking income in the wrong period, or even to outright fiction. In either case, institutions or individuals who rely on these statements can lose money.

The temptation often arises because the managers did not pay enough attention to the capital budgeting process and managing their cash flow. Suddenly, the business hits a rough patch and the need for cash is immediate. A bit of foresight and some capital budgeting can avoid this situation. Unless you have specific finance duties, you will probably only have data input into capital budgeting. But you should understand the process. As you rise in the company, capital financing will increase in importance.

Capital Budgeting Process

To estimate how much cash a business will need over a given period, finance managers generate a capital budget. The first step is to forecast sales. They then project the assets necessary to support that sales level. Next, they decide whether those assets exist presently or if they need to acquire them. Can the assets be supported through internal funds or will outside cash be needed? If outside cash will be needed, decide how to raise the money. Finally, contact the sources and secure funding commitments.

Short-term capital is almost always in the form of sort of loan. Bank loans are common, but many businesses rely on *factor* loans. Factors buy accounts receivables at a discount. The discount depends on whether the receivables are purchased with recourse or without recourse. "With recourse" means the factor has the right to return accounts to the company if it is unable to collect on them. "Without recourse" means that the

---

The Case of Too Much Cash

Smart Managing   Many successful businesses, for various reasons, don't seek credit lines but hold cash from their fat selling seasons to carry them through the lean. But holding too much cash can also be a problem. Like dollars stuffed under a mattress, idle cash can't earn anything. A high quick ratio or acid test—(current assets − inventory) / current liabilities, as explained in Chapter 4—suggests that the business is holding excess cash.

The business should at least set up sweep accounts—bank accounts whose balances are automatically transferred into interest-bearing accounts or investments, such as money market funds. If there's enough excess cash, the business should also have some short-term investment vehicles.

Each industry has certain standard debt ratios, generally a combination of short and long debt. You should look at how your company compares. Assuming some debt, particularly when you have the cash flow to cover it, can help you grow more smoothly.

---

factor assumes the total obligation to collect the debt. Without recourse brings a much larger discount on the value of the receivable since the factor is taking on more risk. Businesses should never get caught so short of cash that they are forced to sell equity to cover short-term cash needs.

> **Factoring**
>
> Here's how factoring works. A factor (factoring company) buys customer accounts from the company, deducting a discount, usually 3% to 5% of the amount of the accounts. That discount is primarily to compensate the factor for assuming the risk of collecting the accounts. The factor may buy accounts *with recourse*, which means that it has the right to sell the accounts back to the company if it doesn't collect from the customers within a certain time. If it buys accounts *without recourse*, the factor is responsible for collecting.

Businesses have more flexibility in financing options for long-term capital. Long-term debt, like a mortgage or some other form of collateralized loan, is most common for smaller businesses. If the business is an entity that can issue stock, that's an option. Some businesses may also choose to issue bonds. In either case, success in raising money through stocks or bonds may depend on good financial statements, so here again there may be a temptation to get creative with the accounting to improve the figures.

> **Factoring** Selling accounts receivable to a factoring company or a factor, at a discount for assuming the risk of collecting from the accounts. Also known as *accounts receivable financing*.

As I stated at the start of this chapter, as a manager you're going to run across fraud. You may even find yourself under pressure to participate in some creative accounting practices or at least to ignore them around you. After reading this chapter, you'll at least be better able to recognize instances of fraud.

Manager's Checklist for Chapter 10

❏ Prepare for fraud. You and your coworkers may be honest, but there will always be people who try to deceive you for their gain.

❏ If you know the kinds of fraud people try, you are less likely to be affected.

❏ Sarbanes-Oxley increases requirements and responsibilities for public companies financial statements. These effects will probably trickle down to smaller companies as banks and insurance companies require similar documentation.

❏ Internal fraud threatens the life of the business. Know the most common types.

❏ External credit card fraud is a persistent risk for companies that accept them.

❏ Capital budgeting and finance are temptations for financial statement fraud.

Where Will All This New Knowledge Take You?

Congratulations! You've reached the last chapter in this book and the first chapter in your new life as an Accounting Enhanced Manager™. You will need that knowledge and a lot more in the next few years, because there is a tsunami of change coming to accounting rules, procedures, and systems.

Much of what we have covered in this book looks at conditions as they currently exist. But this doesn't mean that what you have learned from this book is obsolete. Far from it. My hope and expectation is that you've already had a chance to use information from this book to understand processes or inform decisions and you'll continue to do so. Accounting skills, in addition to management skills, will make you more valuable to your company and increase your marketability.

The whole field of accounting is changing rapidly and this knowledge will be overtaken in five to 10 years. Here are some of the things on the near horizon. Initiatives like JIT and ABC have pointed the way to analyzing work processes for their value-added component and seeing if steps can be eliminated, changed, or consolidated. The whole emphasis seems to be to move responsibility for this sort of analysis away from traditional cost accounting and more toward recognition of all the aspects of the environment.

The coming changes will have the biggest impact on managers in medium to large companies that have an exposure to global competition. In other words, just about all of them. Among a host of changes in other areas, both financial and management accounting systems will be see radical restructuring. The impact of Sarbanes-Oxley is still making its way through the regulatory digestive system like some great capybara. One of the probable impacts will be to hasten the disconnect of financial reporting procedures from management and cost accounting systems.

New Systems and New Thinking

As we saw in the discussions of environmental, activity-based costing, and balanced scorecard, these newer systems want to expand the universe of relevant information. The traditional management accounting systems are primarily financial in that they're tied to the general ledger in the way they collect and report information. Traditional reporting of such information as favorable and unfavorable variances seems contrived when compared with real-world concerns such as on-time deliveries, reject rates, and production yields.

The world that traditional cost accounting described has shifted. When Andrew Carnegie was riveted on direct costs, labor followed by material drove the cost structure. The relatively small overheads of that period have ballooned to contemporary structures that account for more than half the cost. At the same time, the distinctions between direct and indirect costs and between fixed and variable costs become more blurred.

There is even some fundamental rethinking of the whole process of recording, collecting, and reporting cost activity. Coming under attack is the fundamental theory that, in order to control the business, management has to record and check each transaction in detail. The theory would hold that the more transactions captured in the computer or in the ledgers, the more control management has.

Recent research suggests the opposite. You create control by bringing the processes under control. Processes would include activities from new product development and production to administration and quality control. Initiatives like Six Sigma start to touch on these issues. The thinking is that excellence does not spring from the rote recording, tracking, and checking of each transaction. Excellence grows from analyzing and perfecting every process in the company.

What this revolution means—and it truly is a revolution—is that accountants and managers would no longer be lashed to ledgers. It will have profound effects on everything from performance evaluations to product quality. The disintermediation effect of the Internet is forecast to have a profound effect on business processes. These accounting changes suggest a similar disintermediation in accounting.

It will be interesting to see how fast companies implement such radical changes. The normal corporate tendency is to want to be the 19th team on Everest, to reduce risk substantially. This new approach places great value on rapid reaction. Normally, something like this would take several years to implement. The growing sophistication of large-scale databases and the software to support it may draw the moment closer.

Impact on Managers

One strong signal from all this activity is that an individual manager's skill set needs to be both wide and deep. The old concept of doubling in brass to increase a person's résumé applies here. Since a lot of this change will hit the financial and management accounting structure, having an appreciation and understanding of the related accounting concepts would seem to be useful.

One final necessary thought on this subject. Is this just a passing fad? If I keep my head down, will it all just blow over? I don't think so. The new cost and management accounting systems pick up so many variables that are off the ledger that I think we will see increasing use.

A Story

First, here's a story of how two people used traditional accounting information of the type we've discussed here in their businesses. Let's call them Butch and Bubba. They're small contractors who each got the idea that they could strike out on their own. If they worked real hard and did most of the work themselves, they could underbid the other general contractors in their area. They set up separate operations but kept in touch from time to time.

They both enjoyed good initial success. Then, things started to change.

Butch had read a couple of books about accounting. As the money started coming in, he knew he was going to need some help. He hired a bookkeeper and, shortly thereafter, an accountant. He wanted to use the accountant to help analyze bids and work on his cost structure. The accountant was interested only in doing write-up work and handling compliance issues. Butch decided to find another accountant more compatible with his heeds.

Meanwhile, Bubba's business was taking off as well. Bubba had his wife keep his books. He had always looked on accountants as being rearview mirror expenses with little of value to offer. As long as the compliance filings got done, he was happy. He found an accountant who matched his expectations. Bubba went out and bid on more jobs. Undercutting the other contractors was easy and he started to get more work. Bubba added two more crews to try and keep up. The money was now rolling in and he and his wife decided to have some of the luxuries they'd denied themselves for several years.

Butch, working with his accountant, prepared several bids and lost them all. Finally, he won one. With two jobs now, he brought on a crew to handle them while he split time between sites and his office. He set up separate accounts to handle his growing payroll and construction operations. He reviewed the financial statements from his accountant to make sure the ratios and percentages stayed within limits.

Bubba was beginning to feel the pinch, as he had supplies to buy and crews to pay. The cash just didn't seem to be coming in as fast as before. He bid on more jobs, being sure to be low bidder so he would get job. Now he had to start juggling the progress payments, to pay the FICA taxes. Work on one of the first jobs had stalled. It seems the crew assigned to work on it had been goofing off. Next month, a couple of clients withheld payment for nonperformance. He went to the banks to try and get a loan. His accountant could not produce financial statements because his wife had fallen drastically behind on the books.

Bubba is on the brink of entering the self-employed death spiral. Even in these small details, you can tick off a number of things he did wrong. He did not cost his bids to make a profit. He did not supervise his workers. He was careless in his budgeting and had no idea what his cash flow position was.

Butch, on the other hand, seems to be doing most things right. He's costing his bids carefully so he's not bidding to lose money on a job. He is using his accountant in a value-added role rather then treating the position as an expense only. He looks to be watching his cash flow and capital budgeting position. He's spending some time in the field supervising his work crews. In short, he understands accounting. If the books that Butch read didn't include the one you're reading now, he must have read one very much like it.

It seems so simple—but there are 10 Bubbas for every Butch. That's also why Bubba is working for Butch now and a lot happier. All that intolerable paperwork and daily decisions associated with running a business are behind him.

Key Concepts

There are a couple of key accounting concepts or underlying principles that you should take away from this book. If you can see the method to the madness, you won't be intimidated when people start throwing around accounting terms. Your fallback position is the basic accounting equation:

assets = liabilities + equity

Then, by remembering the debit (left) and credit (right) positions, you can start to figure out most double-entry situations. It should help you understand what's going on when the bookkeeper explains what's happening.

Motivating you to ask questions is the second major reason for this book. As a manager, one of your primary job descriptions is to ask questions. Ask questions about accounting issues, the financial statements, how the cost structures were derived. Theorists have even given this capability a fancy acronym, MBWA. That stands for "management by walking around." MBWA is how you learn things firsthand in a business, not by spending a lot of time in a classroom. I should point out that most accounting textbooks are overwhelming—more than 1,000 8 X 10 pages long, weighing between five and six pounds, and selling new for $15-$20 a pound. You also have to sit through a couple of semesters of accounting classes to even start absorbing all that information. In contrast, the information that you get from asking questions will be more pointed and relevant to your job at hand.

If your current position is as a first- or second-level line supervisor, about 80% of your time will be spent with operational day-to-day issues. As you progress to other manage-

Know the Basics

Smart Managing Whatever your responsibilities as a manager, you need a basic understanding of accounting to perform at your best. The decisions that you make or that come down from senior managers will often be "by the numbers." Smart managers know the basics, apply what they know, and keep learning by asking questions.

ment or staff positions, accounting knowledge becomes that much more important. In these positions, much of your time will be spent analyzing budgets, justifying costs, determining prices, things like that. The need for more secure comprehensive accounting knowledge grows as you take on jobs of greater complexity. This is why it's such a smart move for you to start developing your knowledge of accounting now.

While your own knowledge is deeply important, there should be one other person you can rely upon. In the movie *Schindler's List*, the entrepreneur, Oskar Schindler, is trying to recognize the contribution his accountant, Itzhak Stern, has made to the success of his enterprise.

Schindler: My father was fond of saying you need three things in life—a good doctor, a forgiving priest, and a clever accountant. The first two, I've never had much use for them. But the third .... (He raises his glass to recognize Stern.) Ahhh.

Indeed.

Manager's Checklist for Chapter 11

❏ Profound changes are coming to the financial and management accounting fields in response to growing flexibility in management thinking.

❏ The changes reflect the changes in operational business conditions for many medium to large companies with global exposure.

❏ When conditions similar to traditional conditions prevail, traditional methods are applicable.

❏ The skills that you develop from mastering basic accounting principles scale to future systems.

❏ Accounting skills, in addition to management skills, will increase personal marketability.

Resources, Accounting for Managers

Web Sites

home3.americanexpress.com/smallbusiness/tool/ratios/financialratio.asp
This American Express site explains financial ratios and how to calculate them. It also features financial management articles and tools.

industryprofiles.1stresearch.com
First Research sells industry profiles.

www.valuationresources.com/IndustryReport.htm
ValuationResources.Com is a source for industry reports that list resources available from trade associations, industry publications, and research firms.

www.uschamber.com
The United States Chamber of Commerce offers much information for businesses.

www.dnb.com/us
Dun & Bradstreet collects and collates financial ratio information.

www.rmahq.org
The Risk Management Association, formerly Robert Morris Associates, collects and collates financial ratio information.

www.accountantsworld.com
AccountantsWorld.com exists to give accountants "the power ... to thrive and survive under the new dynamics that are reshaping the accounting profession." The resources are for accountants and primarily for members only.

www.aicpa.org
The American Institute of Certified Public Accountants is "the CPA mother ship."

www.cfenet.com
The Association of Certified Fraud Examiners—"a global, 28,000-member professional association whose members are dedicated to fighting fraud"—is a good resource if you need an expert.

www.gasb.org
The Governmental Accounting Standards Board sets accounting standards for state and local governments.

accounting.rutgers.edu/raw/frmain01.htm
The Rutgers Accounting Web claims to be "the Largest Accounting Web Site on the Internet." It's comprehensive, with lots of information.

www.smartpros.com
SmartPros is a portal for the accounting industry. It features good articles. I use it a lot.

www.taxsites.com
This site is a directory of tax and accounting sites.

www.trinity.edu/rjensen/theory.htm
This site, by a professor of accounting, is an interesting compilation of articles and references, especially for accounting theory.

www.toolkit.cch.com
This is a good guide for small businesses from a leading publisher of accounting information.

www.swcollege.com/vircomm/gita/gita_main.html
Great Ideas for Teaching Accounting is where accounting teachers go to get ideas for their classes.

www.cpaj.com/links.htm
This *CPA Journal* site offers several comprehensive pages of links.

www.irs.gov
The Internal Revenue Service site is the authoritative source on tax issues.

www.mywebcpa.com
My site.

Financial Ratios Worksheet from Chapter 4

Since this example was prepared for demonstration purposes and not based on a real company, there are some interesting things happening here. The examples are to help you learn how a ratio operates and give you some feel for whether you may be getting good or bad data.

In these ratios for General Widget, the Current, at 1.5, and the Quick, at 1.02, look low. One of the first things we would want to do is find out the widget industry averages.

The collection period at 51 days and change is running a bit long, but what's funny is the payment period—363 days, almost a year. Then you look and see that you only used the direct materials. There were probably a lot of other purchases. Your accounting software is going to have to be able to capture that information so that all purchases are included.

Ratio	Formula	Answer
Current	$\dfrac{\text{Current Assets}}{\text{Current Liabilities}}$	1,377,400 / 917,400 = 1.50
Quick (Acid)	$\dfrac{\text{Current Assets} - \text{Inventory}}{\text{Current Liabilities}}$	(1,377,400 – 444.400) / 917,400 = 1.02
Net Working Capital	Current Assets – Current Liabilities	1,377,400 – 917,400 = $460,000
Accounts Collection Period	$\dfrac{\text{Accounts Receivable}}{\text{Sales / 360 days}}$	500,000 / (3,500,000 / 360) = 51.43
Average Payment Period	$\dfrac{\text{Accounts Payable}}{\text{Purchases / 360 days}}$	580,000 / (575,000 / 360) = 363.13
Fixed Assets Turnover	$\dfrac{\text{Sales}}{\text{Fixed Assets}}$	3,500,000 / 3,800,000 = .92
Total Asset Turnover	$\dfrac{\text{Sales}}{\text{Total Assets}}$	3,500,000 / 5,177,400 = .68
Inventory Turnover	$\dfrac{\text{Cost of Goods Sold}}{\text{Total Inventory}}$	1,450,000 / 444,400 = 3.26
Inventory to Net Working Capital	$\dfrac{\text{Inventory}}{\text{Net Working Capital}}$	444,400 / 460,000 = .97
Debt-to-Assets	$\dfrac{\text{Total Liabilities}}{\text{Total Assets}}$	3,267,400 / 5,177,400 = .63
Debt-to-Equity	$\dfrac{\text{Long-Term Debt}}{\text{Total Equity}}$	2,000,000 / 5,177,400 = .39
Times Interest Earned	$\dfrac{\text{EBIT}}{\text{Interest}}$	1,150,000 / 75,000 = 14.00
Gross Profit Margin	$\dfrac{\text{Sales - Cost of Goods Sold}}{\text{Sales}}$	(3,500,000 – 1,450,000) / 3,500,000 = .59
Operating Profit Margin	$\dfrac{\text{EBIT}}{\text{Sales}}$	1,150,000 / 3,500,000 = .33
Net Profit Margin	$\dfrac{\text{Net Profit}}{\text{Sales}}$	693,000 / 3,500,000 = .20
Return on Investment	Total Assets Turnover x Net Profit Margin	(3,500,000 / 5,177,400) x (693,000 / 3,500,000) = .13
Return on Equity	$\dfrac{\text{Net Profit}}{\text{Shareholder Equity}}$	693,000 / 1,910,000 = .36

All the turnover numbers are meaningless by themselves. You need industry averages to give these figures significance. You might guess from only a little more than three inventory turns in a year that GW's widgets are pricey.

About the only thing that gives you a rough feel for GW is the various profitably ratios. If you have a general idea of how the economy and markets are moving, GW's profitability ratios are probably pretty good.

If we try to get a picture of GW from just this ratio analysis in a vacuum, we're unlikely to glean any significant information. Couple these raw numbers with industry or internal performance comparisons and you have the makings of some management performance indicators.

Also, one of the beauties of ratios is that you can develop your own if you find a significant correlation between two numbers.

Here's an example. Let's say that I'm a CFO who wonders about the relationship between net working capital and gross revenue. So I develop a NWC ratio:

net working capital / gross revenue

Then I check this ratio for validity. If it's valid, I use it to help manage GW's financing activities. But if it's meaningless, I drop it.

So I observe companies that I consider good and I find that they all have a NWC ratio between 10% and 20%. Less than 10% and you risk getting caught short; more than 20% and you're making inefficient use of capital. I might decide that an NWC ratio of 15% seems best. I calculate the NWC ratio for General Widget, with a net working capital of $460,000 and a gross revenue of $3,500,000 and find that it's a little under 15%.

You have to play with ratios a little—and remember that they offer rough guidelines, no magic formulas. But a wise manager can know a lot about the financial present and future of a company by analyzing financial ratios.

Index